FROM MIRROR TO POWER

A GUIDE TO LOVING YOURSELF

AF651424

BHUVANA SESHAN

Clever Fox®
PUBLISHING
Chennai • Bangalore

CLEVER FOX PUBLISHING
Chennai, India

Published by CLEVER FOX PUBLISHING 2026
Copyright © Bhuvana Seshan 2026

All Rights Reserved.
ISBN: 978-93-7500-203-1

This book has been published with all reasonable efforts taken to make the material error-free after the consent of the author. No part of this book shall be used, reproduced in any manner whatsoever without written permission from the author, except in the case of brief quotations embodied in critical articles and reviews.

The Author of this book is solely responsible and liable for its content including but not limited to the views, representations, descriptions, statements, information, opinions and references ["Content"]. The Content of this book shall not constitute or be construed or deemed to reflect the opinion or expression of the Publisher or Editor. Neither the Publisher nor Editor endorse or approve the Content of this book or guarantee the reliability, accuracy or completeness of the Content published herein and do not make any representations or warranties of any kind, express or implied, including but not limited to the implied warranties of merchantability, fitness for a particular purpose. The Publisher and Editor shall not be liable whatsoever for any errors, omissions, whether such errors or omissions result from negligence, accident, or any other cause or claims for loss or damages of any kind, including without limitation, indirect or consequential loss or damage arising out of use, inability to use, or about the reliability, accuracy or sufficiency of the information contained in this book.

Dedications

This book is dedicated to my mentor, my leader and my inspiration Mr. Kamal Haasan, Member of Parliament, President of Makkal Needhi Maiam and an actor who is the epitome of cinema.

Remembering my father, my Guru and a prolific writer Mr. T. V. Anantarama Seshan with gratitude.

CONTENTS

PREFACE

This book is dedicated to all those who have forgotten to put themselves first; who have lost themselves in the melee of life.

In the hurried swirl of modern life, where minutes often dissolve into hours spent racing between obligations and screens, there is a quiet invitation waiting patiently for us—a gentle call to slow down, to breathe deeply, and to truly notice the delicate details of our everyday existence.

This book emerges from this very space, born out of a yearning to reconnect with the small, shimmering moments that shine quietly beneath the surface of our busy days, unnoticed yet profoundly transformative. This book is an embrace, an invitation to step softly back into the present, to listen attentively to the subtle music that plays in the background of our lives: the rustling leaves, the soft warmth of sunlight on skin, the tender curve of a stranger's smile. These seemingly ordinary fragments, when held with mindful awareness, become powerful threads weaving a profound tapestry of love, resilience, and joy.

As you turn these pages, you will be accompanied by a gentle guide—a voice that seeks neither to lecture nor to overwhelm, but rather to walk alongside you with kindness and reflection. Together, we will explore the art of Self Love, not as a grand, elusive ideal but as a tender habit of embracing life's small gifts.

This journey begins with mindfulness, the foundational practice of learning to be fully present. Throughout the chapters that follow, you will encounter stories that evoke the heart, scientific insights that stimulate the mind, and practical exercises designed to cultivate a daily practice of self-love.

If you find yourself seeking solace amidst overwhelm, if you yearn to reconnect with a sense of wonder and ease, if you long for a voice that meets you with kindness and insight—then this book is for you.

May the whispers you hear in these words awaken your heart, soften your burdens, and invite you into a vibrant, connected, and deeply thankful way of living. May you come to cherish each moment as a sacred gift, and through this appreciation, discover a wellspring of joy and peace that sustains you, no matter where your journey leads? Welcome to this exploration of life's subtle magic.

Learn to love yourself, put yourself forward, and achieve those beautiful dreams that you have carried in your heart all these years.

Equip yourself with a notebook, pen, 30 minutes of your space and time, and a bottle of water. Be ready to fall in love with yourself with this powerful guide. Let's begin!

Finally, this book is just the beginning, a doorway to a lifelong practice of self-love and authentic success. This book is designed to build momentum and confidence, but the real magic happens when you carry these tools into your everyday life, evolving and adapting them as you grow.

Remember, loving yourself is not a destination; it is the ongoing dance of honouring your worth with intention, patience, and kindness.

So, dear reader, take a deep breath and step into this journey with courage and curiosity. Let these pages be your gentle guide in rediscovering the vibrant, worthy, and powerful person you have always been. Together, let's build a success rooted in love—the kind that lasts, heals, and transforms.

Welcome to your journey of self-love and success. It's going to be extraordinary.

CHAPTER 1

UNDERSTANDING SELF-LOVE

You are worth the full version of your life!

You are beginning your journey today. Mark this day on your calendar. This day will be etched in your memory forever because you are going to re-discover yourself today. Before we begin, here's a forethought for you to ponder on!

Contrary to popular belief, self-love is not an act of egoistic self-absorption where the self is placed above the welfare of others or the responsibilities we bear. It is not about inflated self-importance or dismissing the legitimate needs and boundaries of those around us. Instead, self-love fosters humility born from self-awareness, enabling us to extend empathy and kindness outwardly with a fuller heart because we are not operating from a place of scarcity or self-neglect. It does not mean indulging every fleeting desire impulsively as though avoiding discomfort at any cost were the path to happiness. It just means you are not ignoring yourself.

At a deeper psychological level, self-love can be seen as a conscious realignment of one's inner dialogue and belief systems. For many, the journey toward self-love begins by unraveling layers of conditioning, negative self-talk, and internalized messages inherited from family, culture, or society that erode a person's innate sense of worth. The cultural lens through which we view success and worthiness can also obscure the meaning and importance of self-love. Societal messages often equate value with external accomplishments, productivity, or appearance, implicitly suggesting that self-love is something to be earned only after meeting certain criteria. These narratives create traps of conditional self-worth that tether our confidence to passing achievements or approval. Such an approach is inherently unstable and exhausting, as external variables are unpredictable and often outside our control. In contrast, self-love invites a radical redefinition—one where worth is inherent and unconditional, existing before and beyond external success or failure. This reframing is not always easy because it asks us to unlearn deeply ingrained patterns and cultural scripts. Yet, embracing unconditional self-love lays a much sturdier foundation where true success can emerge organically, rooted in authenticity rather than perfection.

The transformative potential of self-love also lies in how it reshapes our relationship with failure and imperfection. Most cultures impose harsh judgments on mistakes, promoting avoidance of failure as the path to success.

This mindset fosters fear, self-criticism, and avoidance behaviors that undermine growth. Self-love, by contrast, invites embracing imperfection and fallibility as natural and necessary aspects of being human. It encourages a stance of curiosity rather than condemnation, where errors become lessons rather than indictments. Learning to meet oneself with kindness in moments of struggle cultivates the resilience and confidence needed to take risks and pursue meaningful goals. This perspective profoundly shifts the internal narrative from one of scarcity and fear to abundance and courage.

Self-love transforms setbacks from sources of shame into opportunities for self-compassionate learning and renewal.

You know what breaks my heart? Brilliant people talking about their dreams in past tense. That's so heartbreaking.

"I wanted to…"

"I used to think I could…"

"I had this idea once…"

As if dreams are a phase.

As if ambition has an expiry date.

As if worth has a deadline.

But you know what? It's never too late. Every beginning is a celebration, whenever you begin it!

A dream is not a random fantasy.

It is a whisper from the deepest, most honest part of you.

When you keep thinking about writing that book…

Starting that workshop…

Learning that language…

Speaking on that stage…

It's not ego.

It's alignment.

Begin with the present moment. Where are you now? What are you now? You don't need monumental milestones to impress yourself, but when you look back, you will realise that your journey has been phenomenal.

Think of yourself as a child. What do you remember? Do you remember a pretty little girl in a skirt? Do you remember a bubbly boy running around? Write 3 words that come to your mind when you recall your childhood.

I, ----------(your name) recall my childhood as being

1.

2.

3.

Those 3 things that came to your mind are actually the forces that shaped you! Think about it! Let me tell you what shaped me. My 3 points were lonely, spirited, and loaded with love. I was a lonely child- that made me independent. I was full of spirit – that made me explore everything that came my way! I had so much love to give- that made me an empath! So begin your story with what shaped you. Take a deep breath, close your eyes, and inhale! Smile! Don't stop smiling, but open your eyes. Take a selfie with that smile still intact. Save it as Day 1.

Reflect on the 3 points that you wrote! You have your story's outline! kindness, your ability to dream, your resilience, your selflessness…. Write them down!

Read them aloud and pat yourself on the back. You are much more than what you have noted down. So, take your water bottle and take a sip of that cool water. Gulp down the realisation that you are amazing.

Finally, write down this :

I am -------- (your name)

I am worthy of all the good things in life.

I have dreams that I am going to chase from today.

I own me! My life!

Your dream is showing you who you are capable of becoming.

And when you ignore it, something inside you slowly dims.

Richard Bach once said, “You are never given the power to dream unless you are given the power to make it come true”. Dreaming is not running behind something. It’s a calling! The Universe is speaking to you. Listen to it.

You are worth the full version of your life.

You have just started your journey. You are yet to be amazed by yourself!

CHAPTER 2

RECOGNIZING YOUR CURRENT STATE

Self-Awareness Assessment

Identifying our flaws doesn't mean you are blaming yourself; it means you are elevating yourself.

Before we embark on the transformative journey of cultivating authentic self-love, it is essential to first pause and take a candid look inward. We must assess where we currently stand, not to cast judgment or measure against any external standard, but to build genuine awareness—the fertile ground from which all growth sprouts. This self-awareness assessment invites you into a deliberate space of reflection and honest evaluation of your self-esteem and habits, illuminating both the nurturing forces and the limiting patterns that shape your relationship with yourself. The act of looking inward with curiosity rather than criticism lays the cornerstone for meaningful change and empowers you to take ownership of your evolution.

In the ever-shifting landscape of life's ambitions and challenges, self-love stands not as a mere luxury or whimsical indulgence but as the solid bedrock upon which true success is built. To embark on any meaningful journey toward personal fulfillment or external achievement without a foundation of genuine compassion and respect for oneself is like constructing a house on sand— beautiful at first glance, perhaps, but ultimately vulnerable to collapse when faced with the inevitable storms of adversity. Self-love is not an abstract, feel-good concept confined to the realm of self-help jargon; it is a dynamic, transformative force that weaves itself intricately into the very fabric of motivation, resilience, and goal attainment. Its potency lies in the way it shapes our internal dialogue, informs our actions, and molds our capacity to persevere amid setbacks, frequently making the difference between fleeting attempts at success and sustained, authentic accomplishment.

Motivation, often misunderstood as an external spark ignited by rewards or the pressure of deadlines, finds its deepest and most sustainable source within the heart's quiet place of self-acceptance and encouragement. When we possess a robust sense of self-love, the motivation that propels us forward is not tethered exclusively to external validation or superficial achievements but springs instead from an intimate longing to honor our own worth and potential. This intrinsic drive transforms goals from burdensome obligations into meaningful aspirations aligned with our true selves. In this way, self-love acts as a compass, gently guiding us through the noise and distractions of life toward endeavors that resonate authentically with our passions and values. It breeds a kind of motivation that is less volatile and more enduring, for it is not easily extinguished by external criticism or failure. Rather, it is fueled by a nurturing internal dialogue that says, "I am deserving of kindness, growth, and perseverance," instilling a profound willingness to invest effort even when immediate rewards seem distant or uncertain.

Reflecting on the stories of those who have transcended self-doubt and burnout further illustrates the vital importance of self-love. Consider Maya, a once high-achieving professional whose relentless pursuit of external success left her depleted and disconnected from her passions. It was only through embracing self-love — learning to forgive herself for perceived failures and honor her need for rest and joy — that she found the resilience to reinvent her career and realign her goals. Or James, who struggled for years with crippling self-criticism that stifled his creativity and confidence. When he began practicing daily self-compassion exercises and reframed his inner narrative, he unlocked a wellspring of motivation that propelled him toward launching a fulfilling entrepreneurial venture. These narratives resonate because they mirror the universal human tension between striving and self-care, making clear the transformative potential when self-love takes center stage.

The power of self-love also lies in its paradoxical ability to unify seemingly opposing forces within us.

Having said that, let's work on our inner self, Day 2:

Sometimes it is important to open up what we have blocked. Often, we ignore our flaws, and we would like to believe that we are beyond imperfections. But, over the years, we have accumulated so many imperfections just because we have been refusing to acknowledge them. **Identifying our flaws doesn't mean you are blaming yourself; it means you are elevating yourself**.

Here are 5 strong mirror questions for you! Ask yourself these questions, one at a time, and write down the HONEST answer that your inner self gives you.

1. **If someone behaved exactly the way I behave, would I admire them or avoid them?**
   This question asks us to step outside ourselves and observe our behavior honestly. Imagine meeting someone who speaks, reacts, and treats others exactly the way you do. Would you feel comfortable, respected, and inspired by them or would you slowly distance yourself? If the answer makes you uneasy, it may reveal certain attitudes that require reflection and tweaking. Write down the answer and reflect on it.

Work on how to improve your attitude. Remember, identifying our imperfections is the key to self-improvement.

2. **Have I ever hurt someone and later convinced myself that they deserved it?**

   We often justify our actions. Sometimes, the heart tells us that maybe what we did was not appropriate, but we brush it off by justifying our actions. We convince ourselves that "they deserved it". Reflect on whether your reaction came from pain, ego or genuine fairness. Replace those with patience, empathy and honesty. You are not blaming yourself; you are accepting responsibility. True growth begins from acknowledging our mistakes and responding appropriately from then on.

3. **Have I played victim in situations where I had the power to act differently?**

   In many situations, we have choices—the choice of speaking up, setting a boundary, or taking a different course. But it is easier to play the victim. Recognising this is not about being disappointed with ourselves. Recognising this is to get back the power of right action at the right time. It helps us to realise where our own strength lies.

4. **When I say "I am too busy", is it really a lack of time or a lack of priority?**

   Busy is often a mask worn by misplaced priorities. Reflect on whether the things you claim to have no time for are actually the things you hesitate to prioritise. Time is limited for everyone, but priorities reveal what truly matters to us. When we recognize this, we become more honest about our choices.

5. **Do I secretly judge people for the same flaws that I hide in myself?**

   What irritates us in others often reveals something unresolved within us. Most times, the traits that irritate us the most in others are the ones we struggle with in ourselves. Judging others can become a way to avoid confronting ourselves. Confront yourself! Be bold and accept your harsh judgments and promise yourself to wriggle yourself away from that! Well Done! Give yourself a loving pat on the back! You have just re-discovered yourself, and kudos to your courage and honesty!

CHAPTER 3

THE BEAUTY OF BEING MINDFUL

Mindfulness is the art of noticing life before it slips past

In moments of emotional upheaval or overwhelming self-criticism, mindfulness acts as an anchor that prevents you from being swept away by the surge of negative feelings. By returning again and again to the breath, bodily sensations, or the mindful naming of thoughts, you regain control over your inner world. This gradual mastery not only reduces stress and anxiety but also builds emotional resilience, a crucial foundation for sustained self-love and success. You come to embody the understanding that you are more than your emotions or circumstances; you are the observer and steward of your inner experience, capable of responding with deliberate care and positivity. The beauty of mindfulness practices lies in their accessibility and adaptability. They require no special equipment, elaborate settings, or specific religious affiliations—only your willingness to commit to showing up for yourself with open curiosity and patience. Whether practiced in a crowded café, a quiet bedroom, or a bustling park, these techniques invite you to carve out precious moments of connection with your own being. And as you nurture this relationship, you strengthen the very foundation upon which your success is defined not merely as external accomplishment but as authentic fulfillment—can be built.

Ultimately, mindfulness practices draw you into a loving dialogue with yourself, transforming self-love from an abstract ideal into a living, breathed experience. By cultivating presence, reducing judgment, and harnessing affirmations as tools of empowerment, you forge a compassionate inner sanctuary that supports every step of your journey. This sanctuary is a wellspring of strength and wisdom from which sustainable confidence, clarity, and joy emerge. In embracing mindfulness, you gift yourself the profound freedom of being fully and lovingly present, a freedom that becomes the truest catalyst for success in life.

Using Affirmations Effectively

The power of words—especially the words we speak to ourselves—can often be underestimated in our journey toward self-love. Affirmations, when crafted and used with intention, become not just mere statements but potent tools for rewiring our inner dialogue, nurturing self-compassion, and laying the groundwork for lasting confidence. The transformative potential of affirmations lies in their ability to counteract the self-critical voices that can become so entrenched over time, replacing them with a consistent, loving narrative that uplifts and encourages. Yet, the art of using affirmations effectively extends far beyond simply repeating a phrase each morning; it requires a careful blend of mindfulness, emotional resonance, and a personalized approach that honors each person's unique emotional landscape. To truly harness their power, affirmations must be more than words—they must be felt deeply, believed sincerely, and integrated seamlessly into daily life. At the heart of crafting effective affirmations lies the principle of authenticity. The affirmations we choose to embrace should align closely with our true values, desires, and current state of readiness, rather than being idealistic or disconnected hopes. For example, rather than a generic **I am perfect**, an affirmation focused on progress rather than perfection, such as; I **am worthy of love and capable of growth** invites a gentler acceptance and encourages ongoing development rather than impossible ideals. This distinction crucially prevents the feeling of dissonance that arises when an affirmation feels untrue, which can ironically trigger self-doubt. Crafting affirmations that acknowledge where you are now, while gently encouraging where you want to go, creates a compassionate bridge between self-acceptance and aspiration. It's like planting seeds in fertile soil—each phrase nurturing the ground for self-love to take root, bloom, and bear fruit.

Furthermore, the language used in affirmations plays a pivotal role in how deeply they impact our subconscious mind. **The present tense is a cornerstone**: telling yourself **I am deserving of happiness** rather than I will be deserving imbues the statement with immediacy and power.

However, simply uttering affirmations isn't sufficient for deep-rooted change without the deliberate presence of mindfulness. Mindfulness serves as the bridge that connects spoken words with embodied feelings. When you say an affirmation mindlessly, it becomes a mechanical utterance stripped of emotional energy. The true magic emerges when you combine affirmation with full attention—when you pause, breathe, and feel the words resonate in your body and heart. Imagine saying I am worthy of love as you gently place a hand over your heart and breathe deeply, allowing the phrase to sink in beyond intellectual understanding, stirring a genuine feeling of worthiness. This mindful practice enables the affirmation to permeate the subconscious, where true transformation happens. It shifts affirmations from abstract slogans into living mantras that nourish emotional resilience and deepen self-compassion.

Let's take the example of Sajan. He was his harshest critic. His failures kept playing in his head like a broken record. Day by day, he felt more and more miserable. One fine day, his friends had an intervention with him, and they suggested that he practice affirmations to heal himself. Sajan did not believe in affirmations but he tried anyway. Initially, he felt ridiculous telling himself, "I am healing". His inner voice kept interrupting. But as the days went by, that voice was stifled, and he felt himself getting involved in the process. In due course, the same mind that broke him helped him rebuild.

Another important aspect is **repetition** combined with consistency, but approached with patience rather than force. Our minds are wired to cling to familiar narratives, and often those narratives are shadowed by self-judgment and doubt. Repetition gently erodes these limiting beliefs, much like waves smoothing rough stones over time. Rather than cramming affirmations into a rigid routine, it's beneficial to intersperse them organically throughout the day—upon waking, during mid-day pauses, or before sleep—times when the subconscious mind is more receptive. With repeated compassionate reminders, the mind begins to shift its default settings, and the affirmations start influencing thought patterns, emotions, and behaviors.

Visualizing the affirmation while stating it elevates its effectiveness by engaging multiple senses and deepening emotional pathways. The brain does not always distinguish between vividly imagined experiences and reality; therefore, pairing affirmations with rich imagery and emotion increases their potency. For example, while repeating, **I am confident and capable**. Imagine yourself engaging in situations where you embody these qualities—walking into a room with grace, speaking with assuredness, or overcoming a challenge with calm determination. The visualization activates the brain's neural circuits aligned with these states, making the affirmations more tangible and believable. Combining verbal affirmations with sensory-rich images nurtures a fuller, more integrated experience of self-love and success.

Moreover, incorporating **gratitude** alongside affirmations creates a powerful synergy. Gratitude opens the heart and psyche to positive experiences and self-appreciation, setting fertile ground for affirmations to take root. Before or after stating your affirmations, silently or openly expressing thanks for aspects of yourself, your progress, or your day enhances emotional receptivity. For instance, after affirming I **am deserving of love**, you might add **I am grateful for the kindness I have shown myself today.**

Mindful Walking

Another enriching exercise is to practice mindful walking, a form of active meditation that grounds you in both body and environment. Find a quiet place where you can walk slowly and deliberately, focusing entirely on each step—the lifting of your foot, the motion of shifting weight, the contact of your sole with the earth. Attend closely to the sensory details around you: the colors of leaves, the whispers of breeze, the distant hum of life. Each step is both a literal and metaphorical move toward grounded presence. Whenever your mind wanders to judgmental thoughts about yourself or your day, compassionately bring it back to the sensation of walking. This bridges a connection between physical experience and mental tranquility, reinforcing the understanding that self-love arises not only in stillness but also in movement, in the flow of life itself.

Mindfulness also invites us to embrace vulnerability as an intrinsic part of our humanity. Often, our judgments toward ourselves stem from a place of fear: fear of inadequacy, rejection, or failure. Through mindful awareness, you learn to soften your stance toward these fears, witnessing them with open-hearted acceptance rather than resistance. In doing so, you allow space for courage to emerge, recognizing vulnerability not as weakness but as a gateway to authenticity and a deeper connection with yourself. This shift is subtle but profound; it frees you from the exhausting cycle of defending or hiding parts of yourself, replacing it with a tender embrace of wholeness. To weave mindfulness seamlessly into your life, consider creating small rituals that anchor you in present-moment awareness and self-compassion. This could be lighting a candle and observing its flame for a few moments each morning while repeating a chosen affirmation, or taking a mindful pause before meals to savor tastes and textures fully. These intentional acts become gentle reminders that self-love is found in everyday moments of conscious choice, not only in grand gestures or achievements. Over weeks, these rituals accrue cumulative power, reinforcing a mindset that values presence, kindness, and acceptance above performance or perfection.

A key technique in maximizing affirmation effectiveness is to pair them with **somatic awareness**. Our body holds layers of emotional memory and habitual tension that can either support or hinder our internal shifts. When reciting affirmations, tuning into bodily sensations—such as the rise and fall of breath, the warmth of the chest, or even the subtle tightening or relaxing of muscles—can reveal blocks or affirmations that resonate. By gently releasing tension or repositioning posture to embody confidence and ease while affirming, such as standing tall, shoulders back, and chest open, the body sends reinforcing signals to the brain, which in turn amplifies the internal acceptance of these affirmations. This mind-body connection ensures that self-love is not solely a mental process but an integrated experience that strengthens personal empowerment at every level.

Another powerful method to deepen the impact of affirmations is to share them in communities or with trusted allies. Speaking affirmations aloud within a group setting or repeating supportive phrases to one another builds a **shared energy** that magnifies the effect for all involved. The experience of hearing and witnessing affirmations outside oneself can disrupt isolation and remind us that self-love is a collective human need and journey. Whether in workshops, support groups, or informal conversations, verbalizing affirmations externally reinforces internal shifts, provides validation, and cultivates a network of encouragement. In this way, affirmations become not just personal mantras but communal declarations of worth and aspiration, inspiring mutual growth and resilience. In essence, using affirmations effectively is a multifaceted practice that requires presence, personalization, emotional openness, and integration with other self-love strategies. It asks for a tender patience and willingness to explore the deep inner landscape where beliefs and feelings reside. When done with care and conscious intention, affirmations dismantle limiting stories and reconstruct loving, empowering narratives that serve as a foundation not just for success in external endeavors but for the truest, richest kind of success: flourishing in alignment with your authentic self.

Here is the list of affirmations to practice every day. Feel free to personalize them. Find a quiet place, take 4 to 5 deep breaths- Inhale through the nose and exhale through the mouth. Then start chanting your affirmations. Say them out loud, feel them, visualize yourself as if you have achieved it. Then close your eyes and enjoy the feeling. Revel in yourself. Smile. Open your eyes. Don't lose the smile. Click a selfie and mark it as Day 3.

The list

1. ***I am worthy of love and respect exactly as I am, without needing to earn it.***
2. ***I choose to be kind to myself today, treating my thoughts with the same compassion I give to a friend.***
3. ***My peace is my priority***
4. ***I have the right to set boundaries that protect my energy.***
5. ***I am the architect of my life; I build its foundations and choose its contents.***

Bravo reader! You have set your path. Now keep walking the path and don't look back. Life is waiting for you with plenty of goodies!

CHAPTER 4

HEALING PAST WOUNDS

Identifying Emotional Baggage

In the tangled web of our inner world, emotional baggage often lingers like unseen shadows, quietly shaping how we perceive ourselves and the world around us. This invisible weight, forged from past hurts, disappointments, rejections, and traumas, seeps into the very fabric of our self-esteem, often without our conscious awareness. It embeds itself deeply in our psyche, subtly steering our behaviors, influencing our relationships, and even sabotaging our dreams and aspirations. Learning to identify this emotional baggage is not merely an exercise in self-awareness; it is the crucial first step toward liberation—a transformative journey that allows us to peel away the layers of pain, shame, and self-doubt, and discover the resilient, radiant self beneath. Recognizing emotional baggage starts with pausing to reflect deeply on the emotional residues from past experiences that continue to affect us today. These remnants often masquerade as recurring negative thoughts, inexplicable fears, or disproportionate reactions to seemingly small triggers. They shape the narrative we tell ourselves about who we are and what we deserve. These silent burdens, accumulated over years or even decades, can form a barrier that prevents us from fully embracing self-love and, consequently, success. Thus, identifying this baggage is a vital act of kindness and courage. It demands a patient, compassionate gaze inward rather than blaming or dismissing oneself for present struggles. One of the most effective tools for unearthing this emotional luggage is **journaling**—a sacred space where the heart can speak plainly without fear of judgment. Inviting yourself to write candidly prompts introspection that reveals hidden wounds. Start by writing honestly about moments in life that still stir discomfort or sadness when recalled. Consider the earliest memories of feeling unseen, criticized, or abandoned. Explore events where your expectations were shattered or where you were told something that chipped away at your confidence. Sometimes, the most potent triggers are not monumental but subtle: an offhand remark, a glance of disappointment, an unfulfilled promise. As you put these memories to paper, notice the emotions they conjure—grief, anger, shame, or resentment—and honor each feeling as valid and meaningful.

To deepen this exploration, allow your journaling to extend into dialogues with your younger self—the child who first carried these wounds. (Revisit the exercise in Chapter 1.)

Writing letters as if to that child, offering reassurance, empathy, and protection, can foster profound healing. Speak lovingly to that part of you that suffered without voice, acknowledging its pain and affirming its inherent worth. These letters serve as bridges of compassion, connecting your present self to past hurt in a way that fosters understanding rather than judgment. Through this tender correspondence, you begin to disentangle the narratives imposed by others or internalized improperly from your authentic self-identity. However, identifying emotional baggage is only part of the journey; healing also requires active forgiveness—both toward those who caused harm and toward ourselves. Forgiveness, as misunderstood by many, is not about absolving the wrongdoing or pretending pain did not exist. Instead, it is a heartfelt decision to release the hold of resentment and bitterness that perpetuates our suffering.

Carrying grudges often chains us to past traumas, feeding low self-esteem by perpetuating feelings of betrayal or worthlessness. Forgiveness acts like a gentle cleansing rain, washing away some of that corrosive weight, making space for self-love to grow. Engaging in forgiveness exercises can be a profoundly liberating practice. Start by creating a quiet, safe environment where you can center yourself and breathe deeply into your emotional landscape. Bring to mind the person or circumstance that still holds emotional charge and silently, or aloud if you prefer, express your feelings honestly—anger, hurt, betrayal, contempt—without censoring yourself. Then, gently offer a statement of forgiveness, even if it feels tentative or incomplete, such as **"I forgive you for the pain you caused me,"** or **"I release this anger for my own peace."** It is crucial to remember that forgiving others is a gift to yourself, freeing your heart from unnecessary burdens. Sometimes, writing these statements in your journal or on letter-writing paper that you later symbolically release—through tearing, burning, or burying—adds a tangible element to the process, amplifying emotional release. Equally important is self-forgiveness. Too often, people harbor harsh judgments against themselves, blaming their responses or perceived failures, thus compounding emotional fatigue. Practicing self-forgiveness means acknowledging that being human involves imperfections and that your worth is not contingent upon being flawless. It requires tender self-compassion and gentle dialogue—reminding yourself that mistakes, setbacks, and emotional wounds are part of growth rather than proof of personal inadequacy. Even on days when self-criticism feels loudest, choosing to respond with kindness, patience, and understanding is revolutionary. Reflect and write about moments when you felt shame or guilt, then reframe them with empathy, considering what you would say to a dear friend in similar circumstances. This shift catalyzes a nurturing inner environment where self-esteem can begin to repair itself.

The process of identifying emotional baggage is seldom instantaneous or linear. It often involves peeling layers cautiously, revisiting painful memories, and confronting uncomfortable emotions that might have long been suppressed or denied. This journey can sometimes provoke resistance or discomfort, revealing fears around vulnerability or acceptance. During these times,

reminders of the nurturing nature of self-love are vital. **You are not alone; countless individuals have walked this path**, and professional support, whether through therapy, support groups, or coaching, is a powerful ally worth embracing. With patience and persistence, the act of turning inward transforms from a daunting confrontation into a courageous act of self-care and empowerment. As you progress, it is helpful to mark your journey by recording shifts in awareness, emotional responses, and the emergence of new narratives. Celebrate small victories—moments when you catch yourself reacting with curiosity instead of criticism, or when you consciously choose forgiveness over resentment. These milestones illuminate the transformation underway and reinforce the truth that self-love blooms not in grand gestures alone but in these quiet, sustained moments of mindful healing.

In integrating this practice into a daily routine, one might begin or end each day with a journaling session—sometimes structured, sometimes free-flowing — recording thoughts, feelings, and reflections on emotional triggers and responses. Pair this with short forgiveness rituals, such as inhaling peace and exhaling anger during mindful breathing or visualizing releasing heavy stones of past grievances into a flowing river. These small, intentional acts accumulate meaningfully, gradually unraveling the grip of emotional baggage on your sense of self.

Ultimately, identifying and addressing emotional baggage is a radical act of reclaiming your narrative and your worth. It exposes the false stories that have clouded your self-perception, replaces shame and pain with understanding and compassion, and lays the groundwork for authentic self-love. As you embark on this journey with honesty and kindness, you forge a pathway toward freedom—freedom to embrace your dreams, to cultivate meaningful relationships, and to pursue success defined not by external validation but by the deep, unshakeable love you hold for yourself.

Journaling for Healing

Journaling for Healing is far more than a therapeutic exercise; it is a sacred ritual—a courageous step toward releasing pain, unraveling tangled emotions, and ultimately reclaiming the peace that has long been overshadowed by unresolved memories. In the silence of the written word, the chaos of feelings finds a voice, and that voice is the beginning of transformation. When we allow ourselves the grace to be vulnerable on the page, we grant permission for the healing process to unfold naturally, like a gentle river gradually wearing away the stones of suffering until only smooth, polished wisdom remains beneath its flow.

To begin this journey, it is essential to approach journaling not as a task or chore, but as an intimate conversation with yourself. The page becomes a judgment-free sanctuary where raw honesty is not only welcomed but celebrated. One of the most profound ways to initiate this dialogue is through carefully crafted prompts that invite you to gently peer into the places where your pain hides. Writing about these experiences can deepen understanding, shift perspective, and foster self-compassion. Rather than forcing yourself to relive trauma painfully, these prompts act as guiding lanterns, illuminating specific aspects of your inner world that are ready to be explored, acknowledged, and released.

Start by asking yourself questions that awaken an empathetic witness within:

What moments from my past still feel unresolved or heavy in my heart?

When was a time I felt deeply misunderstood or overlooked?

Is there a silent sorrow or lingering regret that I have been avoiding?

In responding to these, try to dive beneath surface-level recollections and allow the details, emotions, and bodily sensations to emerge fully. Describe not only the event but also how it shaped your self-image, your trust in others, and your sense of safety in the world. Writing in this manner transforms the journal into a mirror that reflects not just the external facts but the nuanced emotional truths that reside within.

Among the most healing explorations is the practice of forgiveness, though this concept often carries misconceptions. Forgiveness in journaling is not about condoning harmful actions or forgetting the injustice inflicted upon you. Rather, it is an act of self-liberation—a deliberate choice to release the grip that resentment holds on your heart, freeing your spirit from the relentless cycle of pain and retaliation. To invite this into your journaling, gently pose this question: **Who am I willing to forgive, including myself, to alleviate the burden I carry?** Write letters addressed to those who have hurt you, pouring out your feelings with unfiltered honesty and without concern for perfection or decorum. Allow your words to express anger, sorrow, confusion, or even the yearning for understanding. These letters are not meant to be sent; their purpose lies purely in the release that comes with acknowledgment and expression. After the flood of raw emotion subsides, try closing the letter with a statement of release or neutral acceptance—not necessarily a declaration of reconciliation, but rather a step toward reclaiming your peace.

As you continue this healing dialogue, it can be profoundly helpful to explore the interplay between your external experiences and your internal narratives. Many of us carry stories about ourselves that were shaped by others' opinions and actions—stories that paint us as unworthy, broken, or unlovable. Journaling offers a platform to confront these internalized beliefs head-on. Challenge each limiting narrative by writing it out in full, then follow it with a compassionate response from a wiser, kinder part of yourself. For instance, if you write, I am not good enough because I was abandoned, counter it with am growing stronger every day, and my worth is inherent, not dependent on others' actions. This exercise gradually rewires neural pathways, helping your mind to embrace nurturing truths over destructive falsehoods. Incorporating mindfulness into your journaling routine elevates the healing potential exponentially. Before you begin to write, take a moment to ground yourself in the present moment by observing your breath, feeling the weight of your body against the chair, or noting the sounds surrounding you.

This simple act of centering brings you closer to your authentic feelings without distraction or judgment. As you write each sentence, stay curious about what arises within you, allowing your words to flow organically, even if they seem chaotic or fragmented at times. Healing is rarely linear; it is a spiral that winds through phases of pain, clarity, resistance, and acceptance. Embracing this ebb and flow is integral to nurturing a gentle relationship with your inner self.

Ask yourself: What new insight have I discovered about my pain? How has this understanding shifted my relationship with myself and others? What is one act of kindness I can offer myself today? These reflections serve as gentle nudges, encouraging you to integrate the lessons learned on the page into the fabric of your daily life. As days pass in your 30-daythis book, consider incorporating gratitude journaling into your healing practice. Gratitude is not a denial of suffering but rather a widening invitation for abundance to enter your awareness. Penning down even the smallest blessings—such as the warmth of morning light filtering through the window, the sound of laughter from a loved one, or the taste of your favorite meal—grounds you in the richness of life beyond pain. This reorientation nurtures resilience and a fortified sense of self-love. As your journaling practice deepens, recognize that the simple act of putting pen to paper every day cultivates more than just emotional release—it births a profound intimacy with yourself. Through this intimate exploration, the weights of pain gradually lift, making room for gentleness, forgiveness, and renewed self-love to take root and flourish.

CHAPTER 5

PRACTICING FORGIVENESS

Self-love blooms not in grand gestures alone but in these quiet, sustained moments of mindful healing.

In the intricate dance of self-love, forgiveness emerges as one of the most potent yet often misunderstood steps. It is a profound act of release, a courageous surrender that frees us from the relentless grip of anger, regret, and resentment. When we harbor grudges—be they against others or ourselves—we carry a weight that seeps into every corner of our existence. This heaviness dims our inner light and constrains the possibilities of growth and genuine joy.

Yet, forgiveness is far from a simple, one-time gesture. It is a transformative journey that requires both tenderness and resolve, inviting us to engage deeply with our pain and emerge renewed. At its core, practicing forgiveness is not about condoning the harm done or forgetting the past; it is about reclaiming our peace and reclaiming our right to move forward unencumbered.

To begin the healing process, one must first turn inward with courage and compassion. Forgiving oneself is often the most challenging act because it confronts the rawest wounds—those inflicted by failure, shame, or regret housed within. So many of us replay harsh self-judgments on a loop, believing that carrying guilt or self-loathing somehow serves as penance or motivation. This belief is profoundly draining and self-sabotaging. Forgiveness offers an alternative narrative: that we are worthy of kindness and understanding—even from ourselves—because we are inherently fallible beings learning to navigate a complex world. The path toward self-forgiveness begins with acknowledging these imperfections without retreating into denial or self-pity. It requires a willingness to sit with shame and sadness long enough to see beyond them. As you write, ask yourself: What was I feeling at that time? What did I need? Could I have been acting out of pain or misunderstanding? Can I now offer myself compassion for that moment? These prompts invite you into a dialogue filled with empathy, allowing wounds to transform into opportunities for healing rather than mere guilt.

Identifying and addressing emotional baggage is a radical act of reclaiming your narrative and your worth. It exposes the false stories that have clouded your self-perception, replaces shame and pain with understanding and compassion, and lays the groundwork for authentic self-love. As you embark on this journey with honesty and kindness, you forge a pathway toward freedom—freedom to embrace your dreams, to cultivate meaningful relationships, and to pursue success defined not by external validation but by the deep, unshakeable love you hold for yourself. Start by asking yourself questions that awaken an empathetic witness within: What moments from my past still feel unresolved or heavy in my heart? When was a time I felt deeply misunderstood or overlooked? Is there a silent sorrow or lingering regret that I have been avoiding? In responding to these, try to dive beneath surface-level recollections and allow the details, emotions, and bodily sensations to emerge fully. Describe not only the event but also how it shaped your self-image, your trust in others, and your sense of safety in the world. Writing in this manner transforms the journal into a mirror that reflects not just the external facts but the nuanced emotional truths that reside within.

To invite this into your journaling, gently pose this question: Who am I willing to forgive, including myself, to alleviate the burden I carry? Write letters addressed to those who have hurt you, pouring out your feelings with unfiltered honesty and without concern for perfection or decorum.

Allow your words to express anger, sorrow, confusion, or even the yearning for understanding. These letters are not meant to be sent; their purpose lies purely in the release that comes with acknowledgment and expression. After the flood of raw emotion subsides, try closing the letter with a statement of release or neutral acceptance—not necessarily a declaration of reconciliation, but rather a step toward reclaiming your peace. As you continue this healing dialogue, it can be profoundly helpful to explore the interplay between your external experiences and your internal narratives. Many of us carry stories about ourselves that were shaped by others' opinions and actions—stories that paint us as unworthy, broken, or unlovable.

Journaling offers a platform to confront these internalized beliefs head-on.

exponentially. Before you begin to write, take a moment to ground yourself in the present moment by observing your breath, feeling the weight of your body against the chair, or noting the sounds surrounding you.

This simple act of centering brings you closer to your authentic feelings without distraction or judgment. As you write each sentence, stay curious about what arises within you, allowing your words to flow organically, even if they seem chaotic or fragmented at times. Healing is rarely linear; it is a spiral that winds through phases of pain, clarity, resistance, and acceptance. Embracing this ebb and flow is integral to nurturing a gentle relationship with your inner self.

Within the healing narrative crafted through journaling, it is powerful to revisit moments of joy, resilience, and hope alongside the pain. Writing about instances when you felt seen, loved, or strong reminds you of your inherent capacity to overcome and to flourish. Celebrate these bright patches as proof that light persists even amidst darkness, creating a balanced emotional landscape that honors complexity without becoming overwhelmed by negativity. As days pass in your self-love journey, consider incorporating gratitude journaling into your healing practice. Gratitude is not a denial of suffering but rather a widening invitation for abundance to enter your awareness. Penning down even the smallest blessings—such as the warmth of morning light filtering through the window, the sound of laughter from a loved one, or the taste of your favorite meal—grounds you in the richness of life beyond pain. This reorientation nurtures resilience and a fortified sense of self-love.

It is equally valuable to leave room in your journal for creative expression beyond words. Incorporate **sketches, doodles, or even collages—symbols** that represent your feelings, healing progress, or intentions for the future. Visual elements engage different parts of your brain, allowing the processing of emotions in a non-verbal, intuitive manner, which can be particularly helpful if language feels limiting or overwhelming. Together, the written and visual narratives weave a richer tapestry of your healing journey. Throughout this process, recognize that healing is a highly personal and non-linear expedition. Some days, your writings will reveal profound breakthroughs, brimming with hope and clarity. Other days, the pages may feel stuck, fraught with confusion or pain that seems unfamiliar or too heavy to bear. Embrace all these stages with the gentle understanding of a compassionate friend. Patience is essential here; your journal is not a race but a patient witness standing steadfastly at your side as you navigate your inner terrain.

In moments of particular difficulty, it can be healing to write about your pain in a **third-person perspective**. This technique 'distances' you gently from overwhelming emotions, allowing you to analyze the experience with more objectivity. Describe the pain as if it belongs to a character in a story: What has this character endured? What fears does it hold? What would compassion say to it? This separateness can shift your relationship with suffering and create space for tender curiosity rather than harsh judgment. Finally, sharing select journal entries with a trusted confidant, therapist, or support group can sometimes amplify healing. While journaling is primarily a private sanctuary, choosing to disclose parts of your journey can foster connection and reduce feelings of isolation. Another's empathetic presence validates your experience and often provides new perspectives that enrich your self-awareness. However, always follow your intuition and boundaries regarding what and when to share; your journal is your protector, and its contents deserve your utmost respect. As your journaling practice deepens, recognize that the simple act of putting pen to paper every day cultivates more than just emotional release—it births a profound intimacy with yourself. Through this intimate exploration, the weights of pain gradually lift, making room for gentleness, forgiveness, and renewed self-love to take root and flourish. With each carefully recorded thought, you build an unshakable foundation upon which your authentic success can be built, one that honors not only achievement but also the sacred dignity of healing and self-acceptance. The path to self-love is paved with words—bold, tender, and true—and your journal is the sacred vessel that carries these words forward into the life you deserve.

In addition to reflective writing, active exercises can help embody forgiveness in the body and mind, deepening the emotional release. One such practice involves guided meditation focused on forgiveness. Find a quiet, comfortable space and close your eyes, breathing deeply into your belly. Visualise the individual or the part of yourself you wish to forgive standing before you. Acknowledge the pain or mistake honestly, but then imagine it dissolving like mist, replaced by a warm light of compassion and peace. Repeat silently or aloud phrases like "I forgive you," "I release the pain," or "I choose freedom over bitterness." Allow tears, laughter, or any raw emotions to surface without suppressing them; this emotional catharsis is vital for authentic healing. Regularly practicing this meditation cultivates a gentle yet resilient forgiveness muscle that expands your capacity to love. Another exercise involves the physical act of writing and burning letters of grievance. After journaling extensively on your hurt and anger, write a final letter that embodies your choice to forgive and let go. This letter affirms your decision to stop carrying the burden. When safe and appropriate, ceremoniously burn the letter, visualizing the negative energy dissipating with the smoke. This ritualistic act creates a symbolic and tangible release, marking a boundary between past pain and future freedom.

In the context of success and self-love, forgiveness becomes a cornerstone for sustainable growth. Holding onto grudges or internalized shame limits your energy, focus, and creativity—key ingredients to pursue meaningful goals. When energy is drained by unresolved emotional conflicts, motivation wanes and self-confidence falters. Conversely, when forgiveness is practiced, you reclaim your power and focus, enabling you to approach challenges with clarity and compassion rather than fear and defensiveness. This shift impacts every arena of your life: relationships become more authentic, work becomes more inspired, and your connection with yourself deepens. Forgiveness fuels a mindset that supports resilience, adaptability, and continuous learning—all qualities essential for true success. As you continue on this Self Love Journey, consider dedicating specific moments to reflect on forgiveness regularly.

Ultimately, forgiveness is an act of profound self-respect. It honors the complexity of human experience, acknowledging that hurt is a part of life but does not have to define or destroy it. By weaving forgiveness into your daily practices, you open the door to emotional liberation and set the stage for an empowered, joyful existence. In this sacred space of release, the seeds of authentic success grow—rooted in love, compassion, and a resilient heart that refuses to be weighed down by the past. Embrace forgiveness as a gift to yourself—a gift that transforms pain into power and frees your spirit to soar.

CHAPTER 6

DISMANTLING LIMITING BELIEFS

Reframing does not mean forcing artificially positive affirmations that ring false; instead, it's about constructing balanced, realistic alternative beliefs that acknowledge the complexity of the situation.

In the intricate landscape of our minds, limiting beliefs often lurk quietly, weaving themselves into the fabric of our self-perception and potential. These beliefs, subtle yet profoundly influential, shape the narrative we tell ourselves about who we are and what we are capable of achieving. Recognizing limiting beliefs is akin to peeling back layers of an old photograph that has faded with time; beneath lie the truths obscured by years of doubt, fear, and discouragement. This process begins with nurturing a mindful awareness of the thoughts that arise, especially those that seem to diminish our worth or restrict our vision of what's possible. Often, limiting beliefs manifest as internal dialogues filled with phrases like "I'm not good enough," "I don't deserve success," or "I'll never be able to change." These thoughts are not mere passing doubts but deeply ingrained convictions frequently acquired through childhood experiences, cultural conditioning, or traumatic events. They silently sabotage our aspirations, anchoring us to a stagnant state long before we've had the chance to fully explore our potential.

To embark on the journey of uncovering these hidden mental barriers, it is essential first to cultivate a posture of compassionate curiosity toward oneself. Rather than condemning these beliefs as flaws or failures, they can be viewed as habitual mindsets that once served a purpose—albeit outdated or now harmful. This compassionate stance allows for gentle inquiry: where did this belief originate? What evidence supports it, and what contradicts it? Through this investigation, readers can begin to differentiate between fact and interpretation, realizing that many limiting beliefs are not objective truths but subjective beliefs influenced by interpretation bias. For instance, a person raised in an environment emphasizing perfectionism may adopt the belief that making mistakes is unacceptable, leading to crippling fear of failure. Recognizing this belief as a learned pattern rather than an absolute truth opens the door to liberating new perspectives.

Be kind to yourself. You deserve it. For instance, transforming "I can never be confident in social settings" into "I may feel nervous sometimes, but I have successfully connected with others before, and I can improve my confidence with practice" offers a more hopeful and actionable mindset. The narrative of self is deeply intertwined with stories of childhood, past failures, societal conditioning, and personal relationships. Many limiting beliefs are inherited or absorbed unconsciously from family, peers, or culture. For instance, someone raised in an environment where failure was harshly criticized might carry a paralyzing fear of making mistakes. Recognizing this origin provides context that the belief is not an intrinsic flaw but a conditioned response that can be revised. Techniques such as writing letters to one's younger self, or engaging in dialogues where one provides reassurance and encouragement to the part of oneself that once internalised limiting messages, can be profoundly transformative. These activities humanize the experience, cultivate empathy for one's own struggles, and open pathways for healing and rewriting internal scripts.

It is equally important to recognize the role of negative self-talk in reinforcing limiting beliefs. The voices inside our heads do not always reflect reality but can become aggressive critics, eroding confidence and fostering self- doubt. Gaining awareness of the tone, frequency, and content of this inner dialogue is a pivotal step. Readers are encouraged to observe when this dialogue shifts into harsh judgment or catastrophic predictions, and then to deliberately respond with kindness and reason. Techniques such as using a compassionate inner voice, imagining a supportive mentor's perspective, or applying humor to diffuse the intensity of criticism help to soften self-judgment and create space for growth. The environment in which one surrounds oneself plays a subtle but powerful role in sustaining or dismantling limiting beliefs. Social circles that perpetuate negativity, judgment, or skepticism can reinforce feelings of inadequacy. Conversely, communities that celebrate diversity, encourage vulnerability, and practice unconditional acceptance can provide fertile ground for nurturing new beliefs rooted in strengths and potential. Cultivating relationships that support and mirror self-love is therefore critical. Readers are invited to reflect on whether their current environments uplift or undermine their journey and to consider steps to either set boundaries or seek out more affirming connections.

Another compelling approach involves examining the emotions that accompany limiting beliefs. Often, beneath the surface of a limiting thought lies a complex web of feelings such as fear, shame, guilt, or sadness. By tracing these emotions, readers can gain insight into unresolved wounds that fuel these beliefs. Emotional processing techniques, including expressive writing, therapeutic dialogue, or visualization exercises that safely revisit and reframe these experiences, can facilitate release and transformation. Acknowledging and validating these emotions dismantles the emotional charge that maintains the limiting belief's power. Building resilience against limiting beliefs also involves strengthening self-efficacy—the conviction that one can influence outcomes through personal effort. This is nurtured by setting small, achievable goals that gradually stretch comfort zones. Each success becomes evidence contradicting limiting self- perceptions and bolsters confidence. Within the Self Love Journey's progression, readers are gently encouraged to undertake challenges aligned with their aspirations, reflecting afterward on lessons learned and celebrating growth rather than perfection. This process rewrites internal evidence, reinforcing a narrative of capability and persistence rather than helplessness or failure. In the broader context, it's worthwhile to recognize that limiting beliefs do not exist in isolation; they often cluster around core themes such as worthiness, competence, safety, or belonging. Mapping these themes can provide clarity about the fundamental fears and needs underlying one's mental blocks. This deeper insight guides targeted interventions and fosters a compassionate understanding of oneself as a person shaped by experiences and striving to heal rather than a flawed entity. It promotes an integrative mindset that honors complexity, allowing room for imperfections alongside ambition.

While the cognitive and emotional strategies outlined cultivate powerful tools for transformation, the journey to unravel limiting beliefs is ultimately a deeply personal and ongoing endeavor. It requires patience, persistence, and self-kindness, as old beliefs may resist change stubbornly like perennial weeds. Moments of setback or doubt are an inevitable part of this process and should be met with understanding rather than frustration. Recognizing limiting beliefs is not about eradicating all uncertainty or negative thoughts but about reclaiming agency over one's internal narrative. It is about choosing to believe in growth, possibility, and one's inherent value despite past conditioning or external voices.

Through consistent practice of these cognitive techniques and reframing exercises, the weight of limiting beliefs gradually lifts, replaced by a renewed confidence in one's potential. This transformation fuels not only personal empowerment but the capacity to pursue success authentically and joyfully. Readers who invest in this exploration can expect to emerge with a clearer, kinder relationship with themselves, poised to embrace new opportunities without the invisible shackles of self-doubt holding them back. The process of recognizing limiting beliefs is the critical first step on the pathway to reclaiming self-love as the cornerstone of a truly successful and fulfilling life.

Challenging Negative Thoughts

Negative thoughts are the uninvited guests that often stake a claim deep within our minds, subtly but persistently undermining our confidence and clouding our perception of ourselves and our potential. These internal narratives, spun from threads of fear, perfectionism, past disappointments, and societal pressures, frequently masquerade as undeniable truths, commands that dictate the way we see ourselves and navigate the world. Yet, beneath their seemingly insurmountable presence lies a vital realization: negative thoughts are not facts. They are mental events, fleeting and mutable, waiting to be recognized, challenged, and ultimately transformed. The journey into dismantling these limiting beliefs begins with an invitation to become curious about the origins and accuracy of these inner critics, rather than accepting their harsh declarations as gospel.

One of the most effective cognitive techniques to confront these intrusive thoughts is cognitive restructuring, a method grounded in the principles of cognitive-behavioral therapy that empowers you to step back from your immediate reactions and scrutinize the evidence behind your negative self- assessments. This process starts by identifying specific negative beliefs that regularly appear in your thought patterns—perhaps the voice that whispers "I am not good enough", or the one that insists "I will never succeed". Once these beliefs are brought to light, the next step involves questioning their validity with a spirit of gentle skepticism. For instance, ask yourself: What concrete evidence supports this thought? Conversely, what evidence contradicts it? Have I experienced successes that defy this claim? How might a friend or mentor view this situation differently? Through this reflective interrogation, the rigid certainty enveloping these beliefs begins to unravel, revealing a more nuanced and balanced truth. Reframing, the art of transforming the lens through which you view challenging situations and internal dialogues, invites you to replace self- defeating statements with affirming, empowering ones that acknowledge your humanity while fostering growth.

A powerful exercise to nurture this skill is a thought diary or cognitive journal where you commit to recording moments when negative thoughts arise, capturing the exact phrasing of those thoughts, the emotional intensity attached to them, and the situational triggers involved. By externalizing these mental patterns onto paper, you create psychological space between yourself and your thoughts, interrupting automatic reactions. This pause allows you to engage in a constructive dialogue with yourself, employing **Socratic questioning** to dismantle the assumptions that fuel negativity. For example, if you catch yourself thinking, I never do anything right challenge that narrative by listing instances where you have succeeded, no matter how small, thus building a case against the unwarranted generalization. Over time, this practice not only weakens the power of negative thoughts but also strengthens your ability to cultivate a more supportive internal environment.

Equally important is the awareness of cognitive distortions, mental errors that skew reality and intensify negative self-judgments. These distortions include black-and-white thinking—seeing situations as all good or all bad; overgeneralization—drawing broad negative conclusions from a single event; catastrophising—expecting the worst possible outcome; and personalization—assuming excessive responsibility for negative events. By learning to spot these patterns in your own thinking, you invite a clearer, kinder perspective to replace automatic despair. For instance, if you notice the trap of catastrophising, pause and ask yourself how likely the feared disaster truly is and consider alternative, more realistic outcomes. This recalibration not only diminishes emotional distress but also allows for more measured and effective decision-making.

Visualisation techniques can complement cognitive work by engaging your emotional and imagined faculties. Imagine yourself confronting a commonly feared scenario with confidence and grace, replying to your inner critic with words of affirmation and calm assurance. By repeatedly rehearsing these empowered responses in your mind, you build neural pathways that prepare your brain to respond with resilience when real-life challenges arise. Visualization, when combined with grounded cognitive techniques, creates a dynamic synergy that bridges thought and feeling, enabling a deeper transformation of limiting beliefs. At times, challenging negative thoughts requires gentle acceptance—acknowledging their presence without giving them the authority to dictate your feelings or actions. This approach, informed by mindfulness practices, invites you to observe thoughts as clouds drifting across the sky of your awareness, transient and impersonal. Instead of engaging or resisting, you practice allowing these thoughts to surface briefly and then float away, diminishing their grip through non-attachment rather than confrontation. By cultivating this mindful distance, you reduce the emotional charge that negative thoughts carry, thereby weakening their impact and reclaiming your sense of calm and clarity.

Storytelling, both personal and universal, serves as another potent modality to reframe limiting beliefs. Reflecting on narratives of individuals who overcame self-doubt and restrictive thinking can inspire hope and provide practical models for change. Within this book, you will encounter compelling case studies where ordinary individuals, much like yourself, recognized the tyranny of their inner critics and embarked on courageous journeys of transformation. These stories spotlight the strategies employed—from journaling and self-compassion practices to boundary-setting and seeking supportive communities—that illuminate pathways through darkness toward self-empowerment. Absorbing these narratives with empathy allows you to identify common threads of resilience and reminds you that you are not alone in this endeavour.

Lastly, it is vital to cultivate a language of kindness and forgiveness towards yourself as you navigate this challenging terrain. The habit of berating oneself for negative thoughts only reinforces their dominance by entrenching harsh self-judgment. Instead, approach moments of cognitive struggle with the same gentleness and patience you would offer a cherished friend wrestling with doubt. Affirm to yourself that growth is a process marked by setbacks and victories alike, and that the mere act of noticing your thought patterns is a powerful act of self-love. Celebrate small wins—each time you catch and reframe a negative thought—as milestones on your journey to reclaiming your inner narrative.

The transformation of negative thoughts into catalysts for empowerment is neither instant nor linear. It is a gradual unfolding that demands consistent practice, courage, and compassion. Yet, as you commit to these cognitive techniques and reframing exercises, you will find that the once oppressive shadows of limiting beliefs begin to recede. In their place, a landscape of possibility and self-belief emerges, where your mind becomes a sanctuary of encouragement rather than a battleground of doubt. This shift lays a crucial foundation for the success and happiness you deserve, grounded not on fleeting external validations but on the unshakeable pillar of self-love.

CHAPTER 7

REFRAMING FOR EMPOWERMENT

The power of reframing lies in unlocking these mental prisons and replacing limiting interpretations with enlightening, empowering alternatives.

Reframing for empowerment is much more than a mere mental trick or fleeting attempt to "think positively." It is a deliberate, profound, and transformative process that reshapes how we perceive ourselves, our circumstances, and the very narratives we tell about our lives. At its core, reframing is about shifting perspective—altering the lens through which we view our experiences so that they no longer diminish our self-worth or limit our possibilities but instead empower us to move forward with courage and clarity. In a world rife with challenges, setbacks, and constant pressures, the ability to reframe our thoughts is a vital skill. It plants the seeds for inner strength and perseverance, which are fundamental pillars of self-love and success.

The journey toward reframing begins with awareness, recognizing the patterns of thought that often run on autopilot and quietly undermine our confidence. Many of these thoughts take root in limiting beliefs—deep-seated ideas that convince us we are not enough, that we are destined to fail, or that we must conform to others' expectations to be worthy. These beliefs, though frequently disguised as "truths," are in fact mental constructs shaped by past experiences, societal conditioning, fears, and unexamined assumptions. For instance, consider the pervasive thought, "I am not talented enough to succeed." Although it echoes persistently, this statement is merely one interpretation of reality, not an immutable fact. When left unchallenged, such beliefs create a cage, confining us within self-imposed boundaries that stunt our growth and happiness. The power of reframing lies in unlocking these mental prisons and replacing limiting interpretations with enlightening, empowering alternatives. Reframing is a deliberate cognitive technique that invites you to step back from your immediate emotional response, examine the thought with fresh eyes, and consciously choose a healthier, more constructive perspective. This process often involves interrogating the evidence for your beliefs, considering alternative explanations and widening your field of vision beyond the narrow scope of fear or self-doubt.

To begin incorporating reframing into your daily routine, it is helpful to build familiarity with common cognitive distortions that frequently distort our thinking. These include catastrophising, where minor issues are imagined as disastrous outcomes; all-or-nothing thinking, which rigidly classifies experiences as success or failure; and personalization, where we irrationally assume sole responsibility for negative events. Understanding these distortions invites curiosity rather than judgment—reminding us that our initial perceptions are often flawed reflections of reality. With this awareness, you can gently pause when such thoughts arise and ask yourself: "Is this belief entirely true? Is there another way to view this situation?" This pause—the space between stimulus and response—is where the power of reframing begins to flourish. A practical and transformative starting point is to keep a reflective journal dedicated to capturing and reframing your recurring limiting beliefs. When you notice a self-defeating thought, pause and write it down along with the emotional impact it has on you. Next, challenge its validity by gathering evidence both supporting and contradicting it.

This act of externalizing your internal narrative breaks its unconscious grip and allows you to see the bigger picture. Then, craft an alternative, empowering belief that acknowledges your humanity and potential. Throughout the 30-day Self Love Journey, you will find exercises inviting you to practice reframing in diverse contexts—from everyday frustrations to longstanding insecurities. One particularly powerful technique is to engage in a dialogue with your "inner critic," personifying that negative voice as a character in your mind. By externalizing it, you can question its authority and respond with empathy and assertive truth. For example, when the inner critic whispers, "You're not good enough," you might answer, "I acknowledge your presence, but I choose to believe in my inherent worth and potential." This dynamic interaction helps dissolve the automatic allegiance you may have had with self- critical thoughts, paving the way for empowerment. Reframing also extends to how you interpret other people's reactions and societal expectations, which often weigh heavily on self-esteem. It is common to internalize criticism or feel pressured to conform to prescribed roles, leading to a loss of authenticity. Through reframing, you learn to discern between constructive feedback and undue external validation. When confronted with criticism, instead of taking it as a personal indictment, you can be guided to view it as information that may or may not be useful, separate from your core values. Likewise, you can reinterpret societal pressures as invitations to reflect on your own desires rather than mandates for your identity. This nuanced approach liberates you from external control and realigns your life with your unique values, fostering genuine self-love rather than conditional acceptance. To deepen your engagement with reframing, it is instrumental to apply experiential exercises that blend mindfulness with cognitive awareness. For instance, one such practice invites you to **revisit a challenging situation** that still elicits negative feelings and rewrite the narrative from a place of strength, resilience and hope. Close your eyes and vividly imagine the event, paying attention to the emotions and bodily sensations that surface. Then, consciously soften judgment and introduce compassionate interpretations—for example, recognizing your efforts despite the outcome or appreciating what the experience taught you. This vivid mental rehearsal rewires neural pathways, gradually replacing fear and shame responses with acceptance and empowerment.

Another layer of reframing involves embracing vulnerability, which many may find intimidating or paradoxical when seeking empowerment. Vulnerability is often misinterpreted as weakness, but in truth, it is a gateway to authentic strength and connection. By reframing vulnerability as courage—the bravery to be honest with yourself and others about your feelings, fears, and needs—you dismantle the armor of perfectionism and self-criticism. This acceptance frees you to ask for support, set healthy boundaries, and engage fully in relationships and opportunities without the paralyzing fear of judgment. In this way, reframing not only alters thought patterns but also transforms your emotional landscape toward openness and growth. As you progress through this subchapter and practice these cognitive shifts, it is natural to encounter moments of resistance or relapse into old patterns of thought. This is not failure but part of the human condition and the rewiring of the mind. Compassion toward yourself during these moments is paramount because self-love thrives in an environment of patience and kindness. Instead of chastising yourself for setbacks, view them as signals marking the boundaries of your comfort zone, which you are courageously expanding. Each time you choose to reframe rather than wallow in negativity, you reinforce new neural connections that eventually become your automatic response, reshaping the very architecture of your mindset.

The true beauty of reframing lies in its ability to ripple outward from your inner world into tangible life changes. When your beliefs shift to embrace your inherent worth, capability, and resilience, your decisions begin to align with your highest aspirations rather than fear-driven reactions. You find the strength to say no to draining obligations, the confidence to pursue passions that ignite your spirit, and the grace to accept imperfections as part of your unique journey. Relationships flourish as you interact with others from a place of authenticity rather than seeking approval, creating mutual respect and a deeper connection. In professional realms, reframing empowers you to approach challenges as creative problem-solving opportunities rather than threats, inspiring innovation and persistent effort.

Empowerment through reframing is not a solitary venture; often, sharing your evolving perspectives with trusted confidants or mentors enriches your growth. Conversation can illuminate blind spots, provide encouragement, and strengthen your resolve. Many find solace and motivation in group settings or communities dedicated to personal development and self-love, where collective wisdom fosters accountability and inspiration. Whether through formal coaching, peer support, or reflective dialogue, engaging others deepens the transformation by reinforcing new mental models and eroding isolation.

In summary, reframing for empowerment is a deliberate, nuanced re- sculpting of your mental landscape that transforms limiting, negative beliefs into realistic, positive ones, fostering self-love and success. As you continue with your Self Love journey, let these reframing exercises be your daily companions—quiet, steady reminders that change begins within, and that by choosing to see yourself through the eyes of empowerment, you cultivate a life rich with possibility and joy.

CHAPTER 8

CULTIVATING CONFIDENCE AND COURAGE

Celebrating Small Wins

Fear may whisper, but courage writes your story. You are far stronger than the stories that fear tells you.

There is an understated magic in the quiet moments of progress that often go unnoticed—the small wins that slip past the radar of our grand ambitions yet carry the subtle power to reshape our inner world profoundly. Celebrating these moments is not merely an act of superficial positivity but a deliberate, impactful practice that breathes life into our self-worth and breathes momentum into the journey toward the fulfillment of our deepest aspirations. Imagine stepping onto a path with heavy boots, burdened by the weight of towering goals that seem daunting, almost unattainable. Each small win is like a pebble removed from that path, a breath of fresh air that loosens the grip of self-doubt, nudging us forward, step by hesitant step. When you acknowledge these slender threads of accomplishment—whether it is waking up early with a calm mind, completing a difficult chapter of a project, or simply saying no to an unkind internal voice—you weave a fabric of resilience that blankets your progress with warmth and clarity.

Visualizing these wins plays a pivotal role in enlivening their power. It is the brain's way of rehearsing success, making the intangible tangible, and the distant near. Picture yourself standing at the edge of uncertainty, hesitating to take a leap of faith in your career, relationships, or personal growth. Through conscious visualization, you replay moments where you dared to try, to speak up, or to be vulnerable—and experienced even the smallest victories. This mental rehearsal kindles the fires of motivation, crafting a mental map peppered with success markers that tell your subconscious mind that achievement is not only possible but inevitable. When mindfulness intentionally focuses on these wins, it transforms your neural pathways, establishing a dominant narrative of capability rather than incapacity. It moves you away from the fixation on "what's missing" toward a fertile mindset that cherishes "what's gained," no matter the scale. In this space, risks no longer appear as monstrous, all-consuming beasts but as gateways brimming with possibility, heralded by those smaller triumphs that served as stepping stones. **Taking risks**—another critical element wrapped in the celebration of small wins—does not mean leaping into chaos without preparation but learning to trust yourself enough to embrace discomfort and uncertainty. Each small win acts as evidence that you have navigated challenges before and can do so again, encouraging you to confront greater challenges with newfound courage. Every act of risk-taking, whether public or private, calls forth a declaration of self- love: you are worthy of growth, discomfort, and transformation. When you honor the risks you take, even those that end in failure, you fortify your inner foundation of confidence. It's a gentle reminder that success is not a singular destination but a mosaic of attempts, stumbles, and recoveries. In this way, small wins become the vibrant brushstrokes painting a portrait of tenacity and hope. What starts as a minor choice to try, to say yes to yourself, gradually becomes a resonant drumbeat echoing with the message that your efforts matter, your dreams are valid, and your journey is yours to own. This practice of celebrating small wins is particularly transformative because it rewires the way you relate to yourself and your achievements.

Society often imposes a high bar for success, overshadowing incremental progress with the bright, sometimes blinding glare of final outcomes. The world waits for the climactic moment of triumph and tends to overlook the subtle, daily manifestations of growth that make that summit reachable. Yet, these message that the effort is worthwhile, that progress is being made, and that you are a capable, evolving individual. This reframing allows you to redefine success not as a distant, abstract goal but as a lived, continuous experience accessible through daily practice and mindfulness. It transforms the journey itself into a celebration, shifting the focus from external validation to intrinsic satisfaction and self-compassion.

The act of celebrating small wins also cultivates gratitude, an emotional state closely tied to increased happiness and resilience. When you recognize even the minor victories—the completion of a difficult conversation, setting a boundary with kindness, choosing rest over burnout—you engage your heart in gratitude for your own capacity and growth. This practice deepens emotional well-being by anchoring your sense of self in abundance rather than lack.

Gratitude ripples outward, coloring your interactions and perceptions with warmth, further reinforcing your sense of self-love. In acknowledging small wins, you are effectively saying, "I see you. I honor your effort. I am present with your journey." This attentiveness nurtures a positive internal ecosystem where confidence can flourish and fears of inadequacy diminish.

Consider the story of Chaya, one of the individuals whose journey through self-love exemplifies the profound impact of celebrating small wins. Chaya had long felt invisible in her bustling career, overwhelmed by competition and her own high expectations. Early on, she treated success as a monumental, all-or-nothing event, which resulted in cycles of burnout and harsh self-judgment. Through the guidance of embracing small wins, Chaya began to track and savor daily achievements that previously would have seemed insignificant—like sending an email she'd been procrastinating on or setting aside time for a mindful walk. These moments acted as affirmations of her capability and worth. Over time, this shift reduced her anxiety around smaller achievements, which are fertile ground where self-love flourishes. By consciously choosing to recognize and honor these moments, you send powerful signals to your psyche that you are worthy of celebration and care too. It is in these moments that your internal dialogue, which may previously have been marked by harsh criticism or indifference, softens into encouraging whispers that affirm your competence and value. This gentleness acts as a cushion, reducing the fear of failure and increasing the willingness to embrace vulnerability—two critical ingredients for sustained personal growth and authentic success. Moreover, celebrating small wins helps to regulate motivation in a sustainable way. Motivation born out of lofty dreams alone can sometimes feel like a candle struggling against a gale; it flickers precariously and may extinguish when facing setbacks. But motivation nourished by recognizing small wins resembles a gentle fire; it may not blaze dramatically, but it radiates consistent warmth and light, enough to keep you steadily moving forward. Each celebration serves as a checkpoint, a personal pat on the back, reinforcing the performance and opening space for creativity and risk-taking. Chaya's story illustrates how celebrating small wins isn't about lowering standards, but rather about building a sustainable foundation of confidence that can support big leaps forward.

Visualization intertwined with this celebration serves as a powerful cognitive tool, not only to imagine successes but also to mentally embody the emotions tied to those victories. It allows you to rehearse resilience and savor the sensations associated with achievement, making them more accessible and believable. The more frequently you immerse yourself in these positive mental experiences, the more your brain upticks the likelihood of actualizing them in your waking life. When paired with intentional celebration, visualization cultivates an emotional environment where risk-taking feels less like a gamble and more like a strategic move guided by self-trust. This synergy unlocks boldness and creativity that can feel elusive when mired in cycles of self-doubt or societal expectation.

One cannot underestimate the **power of ritual** in the celebration of small wins, either. Creating personal rituals—whether it's jotting down successes in a journal, sharing them aloud with a trusted friend, or simply pausing to breathe deeply and acknowledge an achievement—anchors these moments into your daily rhythm and memory. Ritual acts as a bridge linking intention, action, and reflection, solidifying the psychological impact of small wins. It transforms fleeting moments into milestones and chaotic efforts into a coherent narrative of growth. By honoring your efforts regularly and consciously, you generate a habit of self-recognition that naturally inclines you toward a mindset of empathy and encouragement—qualities often reserved for others but essential to practice with yourself.

Therefore, the practice of celebrating small wins is not trivial or secondary but central to the architecture of self-love and success. It invites a radical redefinition of how progress is perceived, measured, and internalized, anchoring your journey in practices that fuel motivation, build confidence, and foster sustainable growth. Embracing this practice creates a fertile ground where the seeds of boldness and achievement naturally sprout and flourish. It empowers you to move forward with joy and courage, knowing that every small victory—seen, honored, and celebrated—is an essential part of your ultimate unfolding and success.

CHAPTER 9

VISUALISING TECHNIQUES

The brain thrives when it receives detailed imagery infused with sights, sounds, feelings, even scents and tastes tied to your envisioned success.

The art of visualization stretches far beyond mere daydreaming; it is a powerful tool that can shape the architecture of your inner world and motivate you to step boldly into the life you desire. When we talk about visualization in the context of self-love and success, we enter a deeply personal realm where imagination breeds courage, and hope fuels action. Imagine, for a moment, the sensation of achieving a goal you hold close—feeling the warmth of accomplishment radiate from within, the smile playing on your lips, the vivid details vivid and alive. This is not just fanciful thinking; it is an exercise in rewiring your brain to embrace possibility instead of fear, to nurture confidence rather than self-doubt. Visualizing success beckons the mind to rehearse triumph, rehearsing scenarios where you shine, stumble, and persevere, thereby making the dream more attainable and authentic. By deliberately crafting these mental scenes, you prepare your psyche to recognize opportunities, to summon courage when hesitating, and to view risks as stepping stones instead of intimidating chasms.

The foundation of this practice lies in celebrating small wins as essential milestones. Often, we discount the significance of minor achievements, yet they are the bricks that build a fortress of confidence. Each time you visualize succeeding in manageable tasks—whether it's articulating your ideas clearly during a meeting, setting a boundary with kindness but firmness, or dedicating ten uninterrupted minutes to a passion project—you lay a firm foundation that empowers you to take increasingly bold actions. Visualizing these small victories nurtures an internal dialogue of encouragement, reinforcing the belief that you are capable and deserving. In this dialogue, the voice of self-love becomes ever more resonant, replacing critical self-judgment with compassionate celebration. This transition is subtle yet transformative because success ceases to be a distant, nebulous concept; it becomes a series of lived moments within your grasp, gradually constructing a mosaic of self-assurance.

As you dive deeper into visualization, it's crucial to approach the practice with sensory richness. The brain thrives when it receives detailed imagery infused with sights, sounds, feelings, even scents and tastes tied to your envisioned success. When imagining yourself speaking confidently in front of a group, try to sense the texture of the microphone, the sound of your voice resonating within the room, the warmth of the spotlight, and the exhilaration swelling in your chest. The emotional intensity you summon during these exercises strengthens neural pathways associated with courage, anchoring boldness in your subconscious. Beyond mere mental rehearsal, this immersive visualization fosters an emotional connection to your goals, transforming them from abstract concepts into tangible destinations. This vivid internal experience cultivates resilience because it normalizes vulnerability and risk-taking in your mind, allowing you to encounter challenges with grace rather than avoidance.

Envision yourself making a choice that feels daring—reaching out to a mentor, applying for a new role, or vocalizing your authentic self in relationships—and notice how the mind learns not to catastrophise but to anticipate positive outcomes or valuable lessons. This mental rehearsal becomes a practice field for emotional fortitude where courage is exercised repeatedly, muscle-like, until taking risks becomes a familiar, less daunting experience. The paradox is striking: the more you visualize facing fears and proceeding forward, the less intimidating those fears become when encountered in real life. Within this framework, another often-overlooked dimension is the strategy of **"micro-visualization,"** which zooms into the smallest, manageable segments of a daunting challenge. Big dreams can sometimes provoke paralysis, but by visualizing breaking down those ambitions into bite-sized moments, the journey becomes approachable. For example, if public speaking terrifies you, instead of imagining a vast auditorium filled with thousands, picture yourself speaking just to one supportive person. Or if building a healthy routine feels overwhelming, visualize simply putting on your workout clothes or preparing a nourishing breakfast. These micro-visualizations serve as confidence boosters by creating a sense of progress and safety, gently expanding your threshold for courage incrementally. When you succeed in these smaller acts in your mind, your real-world actions have less friction, leading to greater consistency and self-trust. This method honors your current emotional state while steering you forward in compassionate yet determined steps.

Moreover, the beauty of visualization lies in its flexibility and accessibility. It is a practice you can engage in anywhere and anytime—while sitting quietly in the morning sun, driving down a familiar street, or before drifting to sleep. This fluidity helps your inner self align continuously with your aspirations, making self-love and courage an organic part of your daily rhythm. The narrative of your self-love journey, enhanced through visualization, also invites you to embrace vulnerability as a courageous act. Within your mental rehearsals, allow moments of imperfection and uncertainty instead of striving for flawless success alone. Picture yourself pausing, asking for support, or forgiving missteps. This compassionate inclusion of human complexity enriches your psychological resilience, reminding you that success is not a binary win or loss but a fluid progression colored with learning and adaptation.

Visualization thus becomes a safe space where you confront your fears gently, acknowledge doubts without judgment, and reaffirm your unwavering commitment to yourself. This shift from rigidity to kindness transforms how you approach real-life challenges, dissolving harsh expectations and enabling you to persist with grace and authenticity. Case studies abound illustrating the transformational impact of visualisation on courage. Consider Daya, a mid-career professional, weighed down by years of self-doubt. Initially, the mere idea of applying for a leadership role seemed overwhelming, tangled within a web of "not enough" thoughts. Through guided visualization, Daya spent weeks vividly imagining herself confidently leading meetings, making strategic decisions, and receiving genuine praise. Each visualization session layered her psyche with confidence, gradually eroding the oppression of fear. Paired with small victories—like sharing her ideas in smaller team meetings and learning to say no to excessive workload—she found herself stepping into the role she once deemed unattainable. This journey highlights how visualization, coupled with incremental action, can extend the boundaries of courage, transforming what was once thought impossible into lived reality.

Similarly, Rishi, an artist long hesitant to share his work publicly, used visualisation to reclaim his voice and self-worth. He began by imagining the feel of his brush in his hand, the satisfaction of completing a piece, the warm glow of someone appreciating his art. Beyond the visual, Rishi infused these moments with loving affirmations about his creativity and importance. This mental rehearsal emboldened him to exhibit on a small scale, endure critical feedback with compassion, and persist in refining his craft. Through this process, visualization became more than a motivational tool; it evolved into a ceremony of self-celebration, encouraging Rishi to embrace risk and the vulnerability inherent in creation. His story underlines the expansive potential of visualization to cultivate not just confidence but a profound connection to one's authentic self.

Stepping outside of our comfort zones with self-love as our foundation is not a solitary event but an ongoing dance that requires intentionality, grace, and trust in the unfolding process. It asks us to honor our pace, listen deeply to our instincts, and embrace both the excitement and discomfort that accompany growth. By integrating small wins, visualization, compassionate engagement with fear, supportive relationships, self-care, values alignment, and vulnerability, we craft a rich tapestry of practices that envelop risk-taking in safety and encouragement. This tapestry becomes a treasured guide as we navigate the complex terrain of transformation, reminding us that the bravest and most beautiful moments of our lives occur just beyond what feels comfortable, and that each choice to embrace risk is a loving declaration of faith in ourselves and the life we are courageous enough to create.

Create your Vision Board

One of the most accessible and powerful tools to start this exploration is the creation of a vision board—a visual collage of images, words, and symbols that represent what you truly cherish and aspire toward in life. Unlike lists or abstract concepts, vision boards bypass the analytical mind, tapping directly into your emotional resonance. As you gather images from magazines, photographs, or digital collections, you naturally begin to identify themes and patterns that reveal your subconscious values. Perhaps you notice recurring motifs of nature, suggesting a deep value for peace and harmony; or pictures of diverse groups of people, indicating inclusivity and connection; or symbols of courage and adventure, signaling a drive for bravery and exploration. Arranging these images intentionally on a board not only clarifies what matters to you but also serves as a daily visual reminder to center your choices on these foundations.

Yet, vision boards alone, though useful, require thoughtful reflection to truly crystallize the principles you wish to live by. This calls for goal-setting exercises designed not simply to tick off achievements but to test alignment with your core values. It is one thing to set a goal to get a promotion or buy a house; it is another to ensure that these goals honor your value of balance, creativity, or service, for example. To evaluate this alignment, imagine yourself having already achieved a goal: How do you feel? Are you proud, fulfilled, energized, or do you feel empty, pressured, or disconnected? Journaling prompts here can deepen awareness, inviting questions like "What underlying value does this goal represent for me?" or "How can pursuing this ambition help me embody my true self?" By consistently linking goals with values, you create a dynamic harmony, where each step forward becomes a celebration of who you are becoming rather than a transaction of success.

Practical exercises to cement clarity around values include writing detailed personal declarations that synthesize your insights. Unlike vague affirmations, these declarations articulate in your own words the principles you choose to embody and the ways they will shape your life. Revisiting your declarations daily, perhaps alongside visualization or meditation, imprints the values deeper into your consciousness. This practice turns values from abstract ideals into living truths that subtly influence your thoughts, habits, and decisions. An additional powerful exercise involves envisioning the legacy you wish to leave behind. What do you want people to say about you when you are no longer present? What qualities do you want to have consistently demonstrated? This future-focused inquiry brings surprising clarity to priorities, often revealing values that transcend immediate concerns and tap into the timeless parts of your identity. It also aligns your current self-love actions with long-term fulfillment, ensuring your journey isn't solely about fleeting happiness but meaningful existence.

In the digital age, technology can support value clarification and embodiment in helpful ways. There are numerous apps and tools that prompt reflection, assist in goal setting, and track alignment with values. However, the key is to use these resources not as shortcuts or substitutes for deep inner work but as aids to bring sustained mindfulness and accountability. Balance between technology and personal reflection ensures your values remain deeply felt rather than superficially noted.

Lastly, clarity about your values enhances boundaries, a crucial component of self-love and success. When you know what truly matters, you gain the clarity and strength to say no to things that conflict with those values, whether they be commitments, relationships, or internal narratives. This selective protection of your time, energy, and emotional space is not selfish but essential stewardship of yourself. It creates a container where your gifts can flourish, where your self-worth is honored and unchallenged.

CHAPTER 10

THE SMART METHOD

The essence of setting meaningful goals lies in crafting intentions that resonate profoundly with who you are.

Setting meaningful goals is a transformative journey that begins not just with ambition but with clarity and connection to your deepest values and authentic dreams. So often, people embark on their goal-setting path guided by external expectations, fleeting desires, or societal pressures, only to find themselves lost, disheartened, or with a checklist of achievements that feel hollow. The essence of setting meaningful goals lies in crafting intentions that resonate profoundly with who you are, who you want to become, and the life you truly want to live. Such goals don't merely serve as destinations; they become beacons of motivation, reflections of your inner purpose, and joyful markers of growth. At the heart of this approach is the time-honored practice of aligning goals with your personal values and vision, ensuring each step forward feels both energizing and authentic. To achieve this, one effective method that has stood the test of time is the **SMART goal technique**, meticulously tailored to embrace the uniqueness of your personal dreams.

The SMART framework is more than a handy acronym; it is a detailed process that demands precise thinking and deliberate intention, transforming nebulous wishes into actionable and achievable targets. When modified to suit personal growth, its five components—**Specific, Measurable, Achievable, Relevant, and Time-bound**—act as interconnected elements that safeguard your goals from becoming abstract ideals or burdensome chores. However, it is crucial to remember that the technicality of the SMART method should always be softened and personalized to nurture your self-love journey rather than enforce rigid productivity standards.

Specific:

Begin by making your goals specific, which means you need to describe exactly what you want to achieve in vivid detail. Vague aspirations like "I want to be happier" or "I want to be successful" rarely generate sustainable motivation because they are open-ended and lack clear direction. Instead, ask yourself, "What does happiness or success look like to me in practical terms?" Perhaps it means nurturing a sustainable morning routine that sets my tone for the day, or building a fulfilling career in creative arts where I feel valued and inspired daily. As you articulate these specifics, you start building a clear mental picture, which paradoxically opens new pathways of possibility and commitment.

Measurable:

Measurability follows naturally from specificity because the clearer and more detailed your goal is, the easier it becomes to define how you will know when you are progressing or have succeeded. This step is crucial for maintaining motivation and celebrating milestones along your path. For example, if your goal is to increase self-confidence, what measurable signs can indicate growth? Maybe it's speaking up during meetings three times a week, or initiating social interactions with new people twice a month. These measurable markers don't just feed your sense of accomplishment; they also provide real- time feedback that helps you adjust your methods when necessary, making your efforts dynamic rather than static. It's important to recognize that measurement need not be limited to quantitative data—qualitative indicators such as journal reflections, emotional check-ins, or the frequency of positive self-talk are equally valuable. Measures represent the waypoints that show you are on the map you've drawn for yourself.

Achievable:

Achievability often gets misunderstood as a call for settling or lowering your aspirations, but its true intention is to keep your goals realistic and humane, nurturing rather than draining your energy reserves. Achievability respects your current situation, resources, and potential obstacles while encouraging you to stretch just beyond your comfort zone in a way that feels invigorating rather than overwhelming. For instance, if you currently feel burnt out and disconnected from your passions, setting daily meditation sessions starting from five minutes might be more achievable than ambitiously aiming for an hour right away. This ensures sustained momentum, as the foundation you build today supports more significant leaps tomorrow. It is within this delicate balancing act between challenge and attainability that self-love flourishes—by honoring your limits and championing your growth equally.

Relevance:

Next comes relevance, arguably one of the most profound components of meaningful goal-setting. A goal devoid of relevance to your core values and long-term vision is bound to fade under the weight of distractions and doubts. To invoke relevance, your goals must resonate deeply with your authentic self. They should answer the questions: "Why does this matter to me?" and "How will this contribute to my overall happiness and success?" This exercise of relevance is a sacred act of self-connection, a ritual that tunes you into what truly lights your inner fire. Let's say you aspire to run a half-marathon. Beyond the physical achievement, this goal might symbolize your commitment to discipline, self-care, and resilience, echoing values that perhaps you have neglected. When the physical training becomes challenging, remembering the relevance—the love and respect you are cultivating for your body and spirit—fuels perseverance.

Time Bound:

Lastly, the time-bound element sets a compassionate yet clear timeframe for your goals, creating a healthy sense of urgency that wards off procrastination without breeding anxiety. Deadlines propel your actions forward and remind you that your dreams are precious and deserve dedicated attention. However, time-bound shouldn't mean harsh or unforgiving; rather, it encourages setting timelines based on your pace and lifestyle, allowing flexibility for life's inevitable unpredictability. For instance, allotting three months to develop a new skill with weekly practice sessions can be a motivating rhythm, offering moments to pause, celebrate wins, and recalibrate plans if needed. Time-bound goals invite you into a dance of discipline intertwined with gentleness.

To complement the SMART framework and amplify its effectiveness, visualization techniques such as vision boards become essential tools. A vision board is more than a collage; it is a sacred canvas where your dreams, goals, and values vividly come to life through images, words, and symbols. Creating a vision board serves as a daily reminder of your deepest aspirations and the path you are committed to walking. As you select pictures, affirmations, and mementos that resonate with your goals, you start to paint an emotional landscape that nurtures motivation and joyful anticipation. This process transforms goal-setting from an intellectual exercise into an immersive experience engaging both heart and mind. Studies show that vivid visualization activates parts of the brain associated with motivation and goal achievement, making your intentions clearer and more compelling. Imagine waking up each morning to your vision board, absorbing the energy it radiates, and feeling grounded in a purpose that feels both attainable and exciting.

Practical exercises encapsulate this philosophy: consider beginning your goal-setting journey by writing down three core values and reflecting on how each potential goal either aligns or conflicts with them. This reflection often brings surprising clarity and even permission to release goals that do not truly serve your well-being. Moreover, revisiting your values periodically throughout your self-love journey keeps you anchored, especially when distractions or self-doubts emerge. Self-love thrives when your aspirations mirror your inner harmony rather than external chaos. Another vital dimension to setting meaningful goals comes from embracing flexibility and the willingness to adapt your plans as you grow. Goals are not static monuments but living, breathing entities that evolve with your experience and maturity. As you progress, you might discover new passions, strengths, or limitations that invite you to refine your objectives.

Instead of perceiving these changes as failure or inconsistency, view them as your journey's natural and beautiful course correction. The capacity to hold your goals lightly while maintaining their essence is a loving act toward yourself, fostering patience and reducing perfectionist tendencies. For example, if your original goal to write a novel feels daunting mid-month, consider narrowing your scope to write a series of personal essays or even just journal entries that still honor your creative impulse. Celebrating such adaptive successes boosts confidence and reinforces your self-trust.

In addition to personal reflection, engaging with supportive communities or mentors can enrich your goal-setting experience profoundly. Sharing your journey with others who value self-love and meaningful success offers fresh perspectives and encouragement. It also creates accountability, not in a rigid sense but as a joyful shared commitment to growth. You might join goal-setting circles, online forums, or mastermind groups that celebrate the nuances of self- care and aspiration. Within these interactions, hearing diverse stories of transformation exposes you to a broader spectrum of possibilities and creative strategies. Such a connection counters the loneliness that often shadows personal change and reinforces that your dreams are not just valid but worthy of nurturing.

Embarking on this path demands patience, courage, and gentleness, but it also gifts you the profound reward of reconnecting with your true desires and nurturing the inner confidence needed to realize them fully. In time, you may notice that meaningful goals ripple beyond your personal life—enriching your relationships, inspiring those around you, and contributing to a sense of fulfillment that radiates outward. And as you cultivate this rich relationship with your authentic dreams through SMART goals, vision boards, aligned values, and joyful reflection, you create not only a roadmap for success but a sanctuary of self-love that sustains you through all seasons. This, truly, is the cornerstone of a flourishing, successful life.

Vision Board Creation

When words and visuals entwine, they deepen the emotional resonance and reinforce your mindset towards success and self-love.

A unique twist in vision board creation lies in integrating dynamic, living aspects. Instead of a static board, consider digital vision boards or journals where images and words evolve with you. Technology offers incredible avenues to infuse your vision practice with ongoing interaction. Apps that allow you to create mood boards or collages can be revisited and updated easily, helping you stay connected to your goals in a flexible, responsive way. You can also create a vision playlist—songs that evoke the feelings your future self embodies—turning your sensory experience of your dreams multidimensional. This constant engagement keeps your intentions fresh and personal. Additionally, consider layering sensory elements; scented candles or essential oils chosen for their grounding properties can accompany your board, linking your sense of smell to your motivation. The more multisensory your vision board experience, the more deeply it embeds into your consciousness.

Goal setting around your vision board should shift away from rigid timelines and exhaustive to-do lists. Instead, view your goals as fluid milestones that honour your growth and transformation. Utilize your vision board as a compass when creating intentions, asking yourself how each goal supports your core values and nurtures self-love. For example, if a central value is balance, instead of setting unrealistically ambitious work targets, choose goals that promote well-being and sustainable success—such as dedicating time each week for rest or creative pursuits. This reimagining of goal setting allows you to move forward with gentleness and realistic expectations, reducing burnout and fostering joy in the process. Every goal aligned with your vision is a stepping stone, each success a celebration of your commitment to yourself rather than external approval.

The physical placement of your completed vision board is crucial for its ongoing impact. Position it somewhere visible and frequently encountered—perhaps near your workspace, beside your bedside, or even as digital wallpaper on your phone or computer. The key is consistent engagement. Each encounter serves as a moment of realignment, a gentle nudge back to your priorities amid everyday distractions. When overwhelmed or uncertain, this visual reminder can rekindle optimism, reinforce your self-worth, and anchor you to your chosen path. Furthermore, consider ritualizing moments with your vision board: a morning glance coupled with a breathing exercise, a reflective pause during lunch, or a bedtime gratitude acknowledgment related to your dreams. Such rituals deepen the connection and transform passive viewing into active participation in your success journey.

Don't hesitate to revisit and revise your vision board as you evolve. Far from betraying commitment, adjusting your vision reflects the beautiful reality of human growth. Your dreams and goals may expand, shift, or even transform entirely as you gain wisdom and experience. Embrace this fluidity with curiosity and kindness. Each iteration of your board is a new chapter of your self-love story, illustrating how your understanding of success matures alongside your self-compassion. Occasionally, integrating new images or removing outdated ones can reignite enthusiasm and clarity. Remember, your vision board is a masterwork of your relationship with yourself—it mirrors your strengths, acknowledges your struggles, and celebrates your unfolding journey.

In essence, vision board creation is more than a task; it is a ritual of self- affirmation and empowerment. It cultivates the fertile ground where your aspirations take root and thrive, nourished by the light of your self-love. By connecting your values, emotions, and goals into a cohesive and evocative visual narrative, you enhance motivation, resilience, and clarity. This practice taps into the profound human capacity for visualization and symbolic thinking, reinforcing the mindset shifts necessary to rewrite old stories of limitation and replace them with empowering narratives. Through patience, creativity, and ongoing engagement, your vision board becomes not just a portrait of success but a celebration of the beautiful, worthy, and powerful person you are becoming.

Creating a vision board is more than a simple collage of images; it is an immersive exercise in self-discovery and mindful intention-setting. When done mindfully, it becomes a sacred reflection of our values, passions, and the feelings we want to cultivate. As we sift through images, words, and symbols that resonate, we learn to distinguish between external expectations and authentic desires. This process gently trains our intuition to recognize goals that align with our unique narrative of self-love and fulfillment. More than a mere "bucket list," the vision board acts

To Power-INDIA.pdf

as a mirror, reflecting the essence of what it means to care for ourselves intimately while dreaming expansively. Crafting a vision board is best approached in a quiet, reflective space where distractions are minimized, allowing the whisperings of the heart to come forward. Selecting images or phrases that evoke joy, peace, courage, and aspiration encourages us to ground our goals in emotional resonance rather than superficial achievement. The intuitive selection process also reveals hidden desires that may have been buried beneath societal conditioning or fear. As the board takes shape, it becomes a visual manifesto—an ongoing source of inspiration and a powerful reminder to measure success by the gradations of Self-love embedded in every pursuit. Returning to this board regularly, touching it with care and intention, keeps our ambitions tethered to the nourishing roots of respect and kindness for ourselves.

Sharing our aspirations and challenges with trusted mentors, coaches, or supportive communities introduces perspectives that illuminate blind spots and reinforce commitment. These interlocutors can help us discern whether our goals are infused with authenticity or unknowingly shaped by old patterns of self-neglect. Through constructive dialogue, we can practice articulating our desires in ways that clarify intention and reinforce the nurturing aspects of ambition. Moreover, collective settings provide encouragement and accountability structures that make the pursuit of self-love grounded goals more resilient against societal pressures to conform or overextend. Importantly, aligning goals with self-love also requires cultivating the Courage to say no—to external demands, opportunities, or expectations that undermine our well-being or distract from what truly matters. Boundary-setting becomes a vital skill in this context, creating the container within which aligned ambitions can flourish. Saying no is often misunderstood as selfish, but framed through the lens of self-love, it emerges as an act of profound generosity toward oneself and others. It signals that we recognize our limits and honor our core needs, which paradoxically enables greater authenticity and effectiveness in the goals we do pursue. This discipline encourages us to invest energy wisely, choosing commitments that are consistent with our values and emotional rhythms, thus fortifying the scaffolding of self-respect.

To Power INDIA.pdf

CHAPTER 11

DEVELOPING DAILY SELF-LOVE HABITS

Morning Rituals

Morning rituals are not merely habits we perform mechanically; they are intentional acts of kindness towards ourselves.

The way we begin our day often sets the tone for everything that follows—a truth that is easy to underestimate yet profoundly impactful once fully embraced. Morning rituals are not merely habits we perform mechanically; they are intentional acts of kindness towards ourselves, small sanctuaries of calm and positivity amidst the inevitable rush of life. When we wake up and acknowledge the moments that follow as our own, as opportunities to nurture not only our body but also our mind and spirit, we cultivate an inner atmosphere conducive to growth, clarity, and joy. It is this quiet, deliberate beginning that this chapter invites you to explore, urging you to create a nurturing space each morning where self-love can bloom and enthusiasm for the day's possibilities can flourish.

Imagine waking to the gentle light filtering softly through your windows, the early silence gently wrapping around you like a warm embrace, yet instead of immediately plunging into the flood of notifications, to-do lists, and the external demands that so often seize our attention the moment our eyes open, you pause. You hold still for just a moment, this brief pause becoming a sacred threshold between sleep's unconscious surrender and the conscious agency of the day ahead. This pause is the canvas upon which your morning ritual begins to take form. It is here, in this natural stillness, that the first seeds of gratitude and mindfulness can be sown. Taking a slow, deep breath, you become aware of your body—your heart beating steadily, your lungs filling and emptying with life-giving air—and you acknowledge this miraculous presence of being. Gratitude is not just about listing things that are good or positive in your life, but is also about honoring the simple fact that you have another day to engage with the world, another chance to choose self-love as your guiding compass.

The power of gratitude lies in its ability to anchor us in the present moment, to shift our minds away from worries about the past or anxieties about the future, and to gently orient our focus inwards toward what we already have, rather than what we feel we lack. By cultivating a sense of gratitude first in the morning, we build a foundation of positivity upon which we can stand resiliently. It may be helpful to think of this practice as tending a garden within—a garden where the most beautiful flowers are not external achievements or fleeting pleasures but the deep-rooted satisfaction of recognizing and appreciating our worth and the gift of life itself. To engage more deeply with this practice, you might consider keeping a gratitude journal beside your bed, where each morning you can write down three things you are grateful for. These need not be monumental: the warmth of your blanket, the peaceful quiet before the world awakes, the promise of a fresh day, or even the way sunlight feels on your skin. Each note is a small act of self-affirmation, gently rewiring your brain to seek and celebrate goodness, thereby opening pathways to a more compassionate and loving relationship with yourself. While gratitude prepares the soil, mindful movement waters the roots. Incorporating gentle physical activity, whether it's stretching, yoga, or even walking barefoot for a few moments, reconnects you with the sensations of your body, inviting awareness and kindness into this vessel that carries you through your day. This is not about pushing or exerting; rather, it is an invitation to listen to your body's needs and rhythms. For many, starting the day with mindful movement wipes away the lingering stiffness or tension from sleep and dissolves the mental fog that clouds focus. It is a statement that you value your body as a living temple, deserving of attention and care. Visualize the slow, deliberate unfolding of your limbs, the focused attention on each breath as it moves through you, the expansion of your chest, the grounding sensation of your feet connecting with the earth. These simple acts are profoundly healing, reminding you that your body and mind are intrinsically connected and that nourishing one inevitably nourishes the other.

Conscious breathing practices, such as deep diaphragmatic breathing or alternate nostril breathing, can significantly enhance the clarity and calm with which we approach our day. Breathing deeply fills the lungs with oxygen that energizes cells, calms the nervous system, reduces stress, and centers the mind. In quiet moments dedicated to breath, we rediscover that we are more than our fears, frustrations, or doubts—we are alive, present, and capable of transformation. Introducing just five minutes of focused breathing exercises each morning can shift your mood from reactive scramble to deliberate creation, a space where success feels not like a distant goal but a natural outcome of inner harmony and confidence.

Another vital element of a morning ritual is the nourishment of the mind through positive affirmations or intention setting. Words have immense power—they shape thoughts, evoke feelings, and influence behaviors. Starting the day by silently or audibly affirming your worth, your potential, your resilience, and your right to happiness can be revolutionary.

Coupled with this, setting clear intentions—not as rigid objectives but as a gentle compass Points—helps you navigate the day with purpose and clarity. Intentions articulate how you wish to show up in the world and, more importantly, how you wish to treat yourself. Perhaps your intention is to practice patience, to speak kindly to yourself when mistakes happen, or to recognize moments of joy, however small. This act of conscious intention is a declaration of self-love, affirming that you deserve to thrive, not just survive.

While mornings can sometimes feel rushed or chaotic, creating even a minimal routine of 15 to 20 minutes dedicated solely to these practices invite a profound shift in energy. Imagine how different the day can unfold when you have first met yourself with kindness rather than criticism, with awareness rather than autopilot reaction. The external pressures and unpredictable events of a day are inevitable, but your response can be softened and empowered by what you establish inside before you even step outside. Additionally, morning rituals provide a sense of consistency and stability that nurtures mental health and resilience. These daily commitments to oneself become anchors in turbulent times, helping you reconnect with your deeper values and reminding you that success is not merely about achievements but about honoring your humanity every step of the way.

A particularly transformative addition to a morning ritual is meditation—an exercise in stillness that invites you to observe your thoughts and emotions without judgment. Meditation can take many forms, from guided visualizations to silent contemplation or loving-kindness practices that cultivate compassion toward yourself and others. Beginning your day with meditation allows you to meet your internal landscape with curiosity and acceptance rather than resistance or harsh self-critique. It's a practice of coming home to yourself, recognizing that amidst the swirling chaos of modern life, your inner sanctum remains accessible, peaceful, and rich with wisdom. For those who find sitting meditation challenging, even a few minutes of mindful breathing or body scan can provide a gentle yet powerful reconnection. Over time, this practice develops emotional intelligence and self-awareness, which are critical ingredients for authentic success, as it liberates you from impulsive reactions and strengthens your capacity for thoughtful action.

Equally important to the content of the rituals is the environment in which they are carried out. Creating a sacred space—however modest or makeshift—is a gesture of respect towards yourself and your intentions. This could be a favorite chair by the window, a cushion on the floor, a corner with plants and soft lighting, or simply a clutter-free surface where you can place meaningful objects such as crystals, photographs, or journal. These physical settings stimulate the senses and can evoke feelings of calm and inspiration, reinforcing the habit as something special, deserving of time and attention. In this way, your morning ritual becomes not just a checklist but a cherished ceremony within your daily life, a moment of connection and empowerment that you look forward to. This mindful preparation teaches you to greet not only mornings but all parts of your life with reverence and gratitude, deepening the roots of self-love.

Prioritizing even a few minutes of calm, gratitude, movement, and intention can dismantle the pervasive cultural myth that productivity must come at the expense of self-care. In truth, self-love fuels sustainable success—it is the wellspring from which creativity, productivity, and resilience naturally flow. When you learn to greet each day with generosity—toward yourself first—it shifts how you relate to others and your work. You become less reactive and more proactive, less desperate for external validation and more content in your own authenticity.

You might notice the difference in subtle ways: conversations feel lighter, decisions clearer, energy more balanced. What may begin as a small act of morning mindfulness can ripple throughout your entire life, shaping a deeply fulfilling and vibrant journey toward your dreams.

It's important to acknowledge that embarking on a new morning ritual might initially feel awkward or burdensome, especially if your current mornings are filled with chaos, obligations, or self-critical thoughts. Change, even positive change, requires patience and compassion. You may need to experiment with different practices to find what truly nurtures you, and there will be mornings when the routine slips away, disrupted by unexpected challenges. When this happens, resist the urge to judge or give up. Instead, gently remind yourself that each new day is a fresh opportunity to begin again. Consistency builds over time through gentle persistence, not perfection. Remember that your morning ritual is not about achieving some idealized state but about creating a reliable moment of love and intentionality where you can pause, breathe, and reset. Sometimes, just sitting quietly for a moment and acknowledging your feelings is enough to reorient you toward self-compassion.

Another key aspect of morning rituals is customizing them to your unique self and evolving needs. There is no one-size-fits-all formula; what nourishes one person may feel draining or irrelevant to another. You might start with simple breathing exercises and gratitude reflections and later add journaling, affirmations, or a brief walk outside to connect with nature. Alternatively, you might find joy in preparing a mindful morning beverage, whether it is tea, coffee, or a smoothie, savoring the ritual of creation and taste as part of your self-care. The essential point is that the ritual feels authentic to you—it resonates with your values, your rhythms, and your dreams. This act of personalization reinforces self-trust and empowerment, vital components of sustained self-love. By honoring your intuition and preferences in crafting your morning ritual, you send yourself a powerful message: your needs matter, your well-being is a priority, and you are deserving of gentle care and joy right from the moment you wake.

CHAPTER 12

MANAGING EXTERNAL PRESSURES

Understanding External Influences

When we observe how certain environments or individuals affect our mood, confidence, and decision-making, it empowers us to make conscious choices about our interactions and boundaries.

In our journey towards embracing self-love as the true foundation for success, one of the most profound barriers we encounter—often stealthily shaping us from the shadows—is the influence of our environment. External influences seep into our lives in subtle and overt ways, molding how we perceive ourselves and ultimately affecting our potential to thrive. Understanding these environmental factors is not merely about recognizing who or what surrounds us; it is about decoding the intricate ways our experiences, relationships, social pressures, and cultural expectations intertwine to construct the lens through which we see our worth. These influences carry immense power to uplift or diminish the self, making it essential to confront and recalibrate them if we wish to build a sustainable, loving relationship with ourselves. From the moment we awaken each day, we are immersed in a world brimming with stimuli—opinions, judgments, comparisons, and demands that often silently chip away at our self-esteem. Whether it's the subtle criticisms from a close family member, the unspoken competition among colleagues, the glossy but often unrealistic portrayals on social media, or the wider societal narratives that prioritize achievement over authenticity, these external voices echo in our minds long after the direct interaction ends. One of the most insidious challenges in this dynamic is how easily we absorb these external inputs as truths about ourselves, conflating other people's expectations or criticisms with our innate value. This misalignment often leads us to modify our behavior, suppress our feelings, or chase goals that don't resonate deeply, all in an attempt to gain approval or avoid conflict. Yet, this comes at a high cost to our authenticity and mental well-being. The first step, therefore, in reclaiming our inner authority is to cultivate an awareness of these influences without judgment but with curiosity. When we observe how certain environments or individuals affect our mood, confidence, and decision-making, it empowers us to make conscious choices about our interactions and boundaries.

Saying no, though deceptively straightforward in concept, emerges as a radical act of self-love in a world that celebrates overextension and people pleasing. The habit of automatic yes responses can drain us physically, emotionally, and mentally, reinforcing feelings of resentment and inadequacy. Developing the courage and clarity to say no does not mean we become cold or unkind; instead, it enables us to cultivate boundaries that support our well-being and personal goals. It is helpful to reframe 'no' as an affirmative 'yes' to ourselves. When we decline requests that do not align with our priorities or values, we are, in fact, prioritizing our inner harmony and long-term success over fleeting external approval. Over time, this practice builds self-trust and teaches others to honor our space, generating healthier and more balanced relationships. Yet, navigating external influences is not solely about managing interpersonal dynamics; it also involves recognizing and mitigating stressors embedded in our environments. Stress, particularly when chronic, can erode self-esteem and distort self-perception. The bombardment of deadlines, relentless social comparisons, societal pressures to perform, and even physical clutter in our immediate surroundings create an invisible but heavy burden that saps our energy and clouds our mindset. Embracing self-love in such conditions requires intentional strategies to reduce and manage stress, restoring equilibrium both within and without.

Navigating external influences with grace also invites us to embrace the concept of selective exposure—choosing deliberately what content, conversations, and company we engage with. In our hyper-connected world, this function is increasingly vital. We have the power to curate our inputs, from news sources to social media feeds, to ensure they nourish our dreams rather than erode our confidence. This intentional consumption acts as a form of self-love, protecting our energy and fostering a mindset conducive to growth. It challenges us to reflect on what truly matters and discard the noise that distracts or discourages us, much like a gardener pruning excess branches to promote healthy blooms.

In conclusion, our environment deeply shapes our self-perception and potential for success, often in ways we may not immediately recognize. Yet, within this dynamic lies the extraordinary capacity to choose how we engage, protect, and nourish ourselves amidst outside influences. Cultivating assertiveness fosters respectful communication of our needs and boundaries, while embracing the courage to say no safeguards our energy and priorities. Simultaneously, implementing stress reduction strategies replenishes our resilience and clarity. Together, these approaches empower us to transform external influences from controlling forces into catalysts for self-love and authentic success. By mastering this balance, we reclaim the narrative of our lives, enriching our relationship with ourselves and planting seeds for growth that radiate outward into every endeavor.

CHAPTER 13

CELEBRATING YOUR TRANSFORMATION

Reflecting on Your Journey

Gratitude grounds us, reminding us that progress often comes in fragments and quiet victories rather than grand leaps.

As you stand at this pivotal moment in your self-love journey, it's essential to take a profound pause and turn your gaze inward with gentle inquisitiveness. Reflecting on your journey is not merely about recounting the days that have passed, but about deeply honoring the transformation that has quietly unfolded within you. It is in this sacred space of reflection that the seeds of change planted day by day begin to reveal their vibrant blooms, weaving together a tapestry of growth, resilience, and newfound clarity.

To embark on this act of introspection is to acknowledge not only how far you have come, but also to embrace with grace the very essence of your evolving self—a self that is richer, wiser, and more compassionate than before. Begin by inviting a moment of stillness. Find a comfortable sanctuary where distractions soften and your inner voice can speak freely. This reflective pause is more than a routine checkpoint; it is a heartfelt conversation with yourself, where judgments are left at the door, and only kindness prevails. Allow your mind to wander gently over the past weeks, recalling the initial days when self-love might have felt abstract or elusive.

How did you feel when you first embarked on this journey? Perhaps there was resistance, uncertainty, or even skepticism about whether changing years of ingrained doubt could truly be possible. Now, compare that earlier version of yourself with the present moment. What subtle or profound shifts can you perceive? Are you more patient in moments of self-criticism? Have you begun to recognize your intrinsic worth without needing external validation? This comparison, not for the purpose of judgment but for appreciation, illuminates the courage and consistency you have shown, even in the face of challenges.

One of the most powerful tools you can use in this reflective process is the practice of gratitude—a sacred lens through which growth can be celebrated and recognized even when it feels invisible on the surface. Begin by listing moments, experiences, or feelings from your journey that evoke a sense of thankfulness. Perhaps it is the gentle whisper of a thought that challenged a long-held belief, or the empowering moment you set a boundary that defended your peace. Maybe it is the small victories: choosing to rest when exhaustion beckoned, writing that honest journal entry, or simply saying "no" when an obligation didn't nurture your soul. Gratitude grounds us, reminding us that progress often comes in fragments and quiet victories rather than grand leaps.

Looking toward the future through the lens of reflection is equally essential. Envision the version of yourself you aspire to embody as you carry forward the lessons of self-love. Paint this vision vividly in your mind, free from the constraints of doubt and societal expectations. What qualities does this future self radiate? Perhaps calm confidence, boundless compassion, or unwavering resilience come to the fore. Imagine what everyday life looks like when these qualities are fully realized—how does it feel to greet each morning, to navigate relationships, to pursue your aspirations? This exercise is not about creating a rigid blueprint but about nurturing a living vision that can inspire and guide your ongoing growth.

Write about this future self in a way that invites connection rather than pressure, honoring the evolutionary nature of personal transformation.

A significant part of honoring your journey involves recognizing the inner dialogue that has accompanied your milestones and struggles. Notice the nature of your self-talk—is it nurturing, critical, or a complex blend of both? How has it changed since you began this journey? You might observe moments when the voice of self-compassion overrides old patterns of negativity, or times when self-doubt still creeps in despite your best efforts. Bringing awareness to these conversational threads illuminates the intricate dance between belief and behavior that shapes our self-love narrative. To deepen this understanding, you might chronicle specific instances where self- talk influenced your choices, emotions, or actions, and then consciously rewrite those narratives with gentler, supportive affirmations. This powerful rewriting opens the door to lasting transformation, reshaping your inner world in alignment with your worth.

As you consolidate your reflections, remember that this is not a fixed endpoint but a dynamic phase within a lifelong journey. The progress you've made is the fertile soil from which new insights, habits, and joys will continue to grow. You might choose to document this reflection through journaling, creating a letter to your future self, or even expressing your feelings artistically through drawing, music, or movement. The chosen medium should resonate with your innermost being, making the act of reflection a deeply restorative experience. Revisiting this reflection periodically can act as a compass, ensuring you stay aligned with the self-love values that will guide you through life's inevitable ebbs and flows.

As you close this chapter of reflection, hold a quiet promise to yourself—to keep returning to this sacred inner space whenever life's noise threatens to drown your authentic voice. Know that within you lies an unwavering well of love, patience, and wisdom, ready to be tapped again and again. Your journey is uniquely yours, unfolding with its own rhythm and grace, and every step taken with self-love brings you closer to a life of true, radiant success.

Reward Yourself

Rewarding yourself is not merely a luxury or an afterthought; it is a vital act of acknowledgment and kindness toward yourself that reinforces the value of the efforts you are making to nurture your growth and self-worth. Imagine how different your journey might feel if, rather than brushing past your achievements with a fleeting thought or dismissive attitude, you consciously chose to pause, to savor, and to celebrate those victories, both big and small. These moments of self-recognition serve as beacons of encouragement that light your way forward, encouraging resilience when obstacles arise, and deepening your connection with yourself by acknowledging your inherent worth and dedication.

In this process of rewarding yourself, it also becomes evident how interconnected celebration is with future planning and sustained self-love practices. As you outline your rewards and recognitions for this transformational journey, consider how these acts of celebration might ripple outward to other areas of your life—perhaps inspiring you to build rituals for family gatherings, create moments of appreciation with friends, or infuse your workplace with small acts of recognition for yourself and colleagues. When self-love broadens into community celebration, it multiplies impact, fostering environments where everyone feels valued and motivated. Yet always, the heart of reward remains personal and intimate—an internal embrace that says, "Here I am—recognized, cherished, and worthy. I celebrate the journey I am on."

Ultimately, meaningful celebrations become transformative milestones that punctuate the narrative of your evolving self-love story. They invite you to slow down, breathe deeply, and rejoice not only in what you have done but in who you are becoming. Rewarding yourself becomes an act of reclaiming your own narrative from a culture of relentless striving and external validation, shifting it instead toward authentic joy, presence, and fulfillment. As you continue to nurture this practice, your life blossoms into a series of intentional moments where success and self-love dance hand in hand, each celebration reinforcing the truth that the most profound achievement is the love you cultivate within yourself. In these ritualized recognitions, you find not just motivation to keep moving but the essential nourishment that sustains your total well-being—mind, body, and soul.

Fall in love—with yourself and the world around you! You are worth the journey!

INDIA.pdf

EPILOGUE

Before you close the book, just keep these little things in your mind. You don't have to feel guilty about putting yourself first. Remember, you are not ignoring others; you are just ensuring that you do not erase yourself in the process.

I never regretted doing anything for my family, but I regretted doing nothing for myself.

We are conditioned to neglect ourselves; conditioned to focus on others. Years and years of this conditioning yields to a lump in the throat one day and that's when we begin to feel bitterness, disappointment, self-loathing—all these surface at once!

Learn to love yourself. Learn to put yourself as a priority. Be available for yourself too! Show up for yourself! The minute you abandon yourself, people stop seeing you. Your dreams are not an inconvenience. They were placed inside you for a reason. The impulse to create, talk, develop, study again, start anew, and grow is holy. When you neglect something for long, it doesn't die. It develops into resentment. Into frustration. Into a realisation that "This isn't the life I imagined". **You deserve better than just the survival mode.**

Choose yourself; not just once, but repeatedly! Sometimes you need to speak out. Then you can bloom like that beautiful sunflower, always bright, always happy!

Own that sunflower! Own you!

INDIA.pdf

INDIA.pdf